YOU CARRY THE TENT, I'LL CARRY THE BABY

One Family's Journey on the Pacific Crest Trail

Jack McClure

Illustrations by Cody Markelz

Photos by Jack and Alana McClure

Paperback ISBN: 979-8-9899061-0-9

eBook ISBN: 979-8-9899061-1-6

Library of Congress Control Number: 2024906040

First edition 2024

To Enedina,
who inspired us to embark on this journey,
bringing smiles to our faces and joy to our hearts.

"The woods are lovely, dark and deep
But I have promises to keep,
And miles to go before I sleep,
And miles to go before I sleep."
-Robert Frost

Contents

START

SEATTLE

↑
P
C
T
↓

WASHINGTON

PORTLAND

OREGON

NORTHERN
CALIFORNIA

↑
P
C
T
↓

SIERRA

SAN
FRANCISCO

DESERT

PACIFIC
CREST
TRAIL

LOS
ANGELES

↑
P
C
T
↓

N
↑

SAN
DIEGO

CAMPO
(END)

Prologue

T hree weeks after finishing our trip, I found myself looking out over the emptiness of the Mojave Desert. I felt the sand beneath my toes, having cast away my shoes weeks ago, carefully stepping around the desert buckwheat as I gazed upon the surrounding mountains. Following the end of our journey on the Pacific Crest Trail (PCT), we—my wife Alana, our daughter Enedina, and I—had gone to Quail Haven, my friend Tyler's abode miles from the nearest town in Southern California's vast desert. The transition was about all that we could have asked for, somewhat like a halfway house, away from the hustle and bustle of urban environments, allowing us to continue our simple life outdoors as we tried to make sense of what we had just done.

Enedina, nearing 13 months in age, was becoming adept at exploring wild landscapes. The time on the trail had introduced her to an array of stimuli and plenty of opportunities to help build her confidence in her increasing abilities. We'd watch as she crawled across the sand, undeterred by the roughness of the small rocks. After months of watching us walk on trail, she was eager to set forth on her own. We'd take turns walking down Quail Haven's dirt track, her little hand reaching up to grab one of our fingers. We'd toddle hand in hand, stopping at every desert bush to play with the seeds and flowers.

Inside the tipi where we slept, our backpacks and gear were stashed in a corner, unused and largely untouched since we'd left the PCT. My knees ached and tired muscles burned thinking of the heavy loads we had carried. After months of full-bore effort, with little in the way of relaxation, we luxuriated in our new circumstances, embracing idleness and indulgence, spending our days lying around in a hammock, reading books, stuffing ourselves with fresh produce and ice cream, and watching the subtle movements of the desert.

I'd been naïve about so many things before we set out, thinking that brute determination and our skills in the outdoors would see us through. And while they had gotten us nearly all the way there, our trip had not been without its challenges, challenges that sent my relationship with Alana to the brink, making us at times unsure if we would leave the trail together. Challenges like the stress that comes with dealing with an infant and the sleepless nights that go with it. And challenges like the daily, compounding physical and mental stressors of life on the trail.

The experience had left an indelible mark on us as individuals and as a family, one with which we were still grappling. Our daughter had thrived, we had survived, and the PCT had given us an experience we will remember for the rest of our lives. But as I looked back, I couldn't help but hear a little voice from the depths of my mind whisper, *Was it all worth it?*

1

The Idea

Grand adventures aren't typically the first thing that comes to mind when modern parents welcome a baby into the world. It's a time of doubt, uncertainty, and ever-mounting fatigue, filled with days of changing diapers, figuring out what she could be crying about, and sleepless nights that go on forever. So who in their right mind when dealing with these stressors would think: "Hey, you know what would be a good idea right now? Let's thru-hike the PCT as a family!"

My wife, Alana, and I welcomed our daughter, Enedina, into the world in September 2022. Those months prior to her birth were an unusual time of idleness for us at our home in Fairbanks, Alaska. Summer is typically the busy season, with nearly twenty-four hours of sun providing the perfect opportunity to work on projects at home, hike and float the wild expanses, and get ready for the coming winter. Time outdoors has been an integral part of our relationship, and we've continued to foster that by going on packraft and hiking trips over the years. But the summer of 2022 was filled with smoke as over three million acres of forest in Alaska burned. With air quality at horrendous levels, frequently unmatched anywhere else in the world, we didn't roam outdoors far from home. Throughout that summer, I would wander around our garden, the smell of burnt wood ever-present, trying to spend as much time outside as was reasonable. Being pregnant and not willing to risk anything health-wise, Alana stayed inside, occupying herself with books, exercise, and baking.

Being cooped up this way led me to dream. Dream of the life we could live as a family and how we wanted to raise our daughter. For both of us, nature has always been where we find the most contentment. Alana and I first met in 2019, working in forestry for the State of Alaska. Both of us had grown up in suburban environments outside big cities, Alana in Boston and me in Chicago, and rarely did outdoor activities with our families growing up. For Alana, it was trail work that was her gateway to the outdoors; she spent eight years living out of a tent, working with chainsaws, shovels, picks, and assorted hand tools maintaining trails in national parks and other conservation areas before moving to Alaska in 2014. Mine was a NOLS semester course I took in 2013 in Alaska, during which I fell in love with the vast wild spaces. I moved to Arctic Alaska in the spring of 2015 and have lived in the state ever since.

Late in that smoky summer of 2022, I came across the book *All the Wild That Remains*, about Ed Abbey, Wallace Stegner, and the American West. The author, David Gessner, traveled throughout the American West, exploring the places and people that connected and shaped the two writers. The book planted a seed. What if we were to take a hiking trip around the Southwest after Din (our nickname for Enedina, pronounced "Deen") was born?

That trip could be a springboard for the bigger, more complex trips that had sat on the back burner for years. A baby and the start of our family were our chance at living the life we wanted to live, and it seemed foolish to pass that up. They offered the opportunity to reset our lives, committed to living our values and to setting a positive example for our daughter. Pre-baby, we had done longer trips in Alaska by foot and packraft, but these more local outings seemed like something we could do at any age. Then, I thought, what about the Pacific Crest Trail? Alana had worked for months on various parts of the scenic byway during her time on trail crew and had repeatedly said that she was eager to hike the whole thing at some point.

"What if we hiked the PCT next year?"
"What are we going to do about Enedina?"
"She's coming with, of course."
"Has anyone done that?"
"I don't know, but we can."

The Pacific Crest National Scenic Trail is one of eleven long trails in the United States, and one of three that traverses the country from north to south. The PCT stretches 2,650 miles across three states—Washington, Oregon, and California—with its northern terminus at the Canadian Border and southern terminus at the Mexican border. Thru-hiking has become more popular over the years, largely due to Cheryl Strayed, whose book (and eventual movie) *Wild* brought the trail into mainstream consciousness. Each section of the trail has unique challenges that deter most from hiking its entire length. In the Southern California desert, hikers are often dealing with extreme heat, limited water supplies, and constant sun exposure. Then, rising beyond the desert in the middle of the state, the Sierra Nevada Mountain Range (the Sierras) brings high altitudes and large elevation changes. Farther north, from Northern California through Washington, hikers run the risk of being caught near a wildfire or, in some years, consumed by bugs. Collectively, these factors make for a challenging hike, one that only some 700 people complete per year.

Before we could consider tackling the trail, we'd have to deal with challenges at home. Din arrived ten days after her due date via a surprise C-section, making Alana's road to recovery much more difficult than expected. Coming home from the hospital, she insisted on walking the forty yards up our driveway to the house, taking ten minutes to do so. Each day, she continued to move, and after a few weeks was walking as far as she wanted without pain. By six weeks postpartum, Din and Alana were medically cleared. With the doctor's green light, we loaded up our car, heading south for warmer climes.

We spent six weeks hiking around the canyons, mesas, and badlands of Utah, Arizona, and New Mexico living out of our tent, finding a basecamp for a few days to a week, hiking throughout each area then moving on. Din took to camping and life in her backpack/child carrier well. The trip affirmed that we could do all the things we wanted with some slight accommodations for our new addition. We moved a bit slower than before and had to take more breaks, but we found that having a baby with us was no excuse to stay home and only dream of adventures that could have been.

As the months went on, the idea of the PCT gradually settled in our minds, growing more appealing with each passing day. It was obvious that taking infants on outdoor adventures was not the norm, but we were not lacking for inspiration from other parents within Alaska. Our friends Andrew and Eva Allaby had taken their little ones on multiple bike trips over the years, sometimes for months at a time. Erin and Hig McKittrick of Seldovia, Alaska, offered another example, taking theirs on multi-month expeditions, traveling hundreds of miles off-trail throughout Alaska's coasts and mountains. And finally, Patrick and Caroline Van Hemmert had taken their kids in kayaks and sailboats around Glacier Bay National Park and Preserve, near their home in southeast Alaska. All were veterans of long trips before their kids were born who then figured out ways to adapt, incorporating their kids into their plans rather than shelving their activities for something more civilized and localized. If they could do it in the rugged wilderness of Alaska, why couldn't we do it on a trail in far more populated areas with plenty of infrastructure?

Still, we wanted to do our due diligence. A search online didn't yield many results for parents thru-hiking with toddlers, let alone infants. However, we were able to find a couple who took their 12-month-old on the Appalachian Trail for at least a few hundred miles. All we could find for the PCT was a couple who hiked 1,000 miles in the summer of 2022, with three toddlers under 5! That seemed far crazier than what we were doing. We'd be able to pack our daughter along, but I couldn't imagine trying to coerce 3 toddlers to walk up to 15 miles a day. Again, we were left thinking, *If they can do it, why can't we?*

Neither of us had hiked a "long trail" before, but we weren't short on outdoor experience. We frequently hiked off-trail in Alaska and had competed in wilderness races, like the Alaska Mountain Wilderness Classic, over long distances in both summer and winter. I had walked 60-plus miles a day off-trail in the mountains during some of these trips, often through the classic, "character-building" terrain Alaska has to offer, like swamps, tussocks, extreme cold, insane levels of bugs, heavy bushwhacking, glacial travel, and river crossings for up to 200 miles at a time. A particularly grueling experience was a 2016 event, when, after covering 120 miles off-trail across the Brooks Range in 53 hours with minimal rest, I couldn't walk without pain for six weeks. We often traveled by map and compass over routes of our choosing. Plus, our forays in the Desert Southwest camping and hiking with Din had proven that we could do the same with a baby.

Once we realized that the trip was feasible, we started on our preparations, considering what gear we would need, how we would resupply, and how best to keep Din clean, fed, and healthy on the PCT. Early January brought about the opening of permit applications for southbound hikers, and we submitted ours. Not long after, we got word from the Pacific Crest

Trail Association that we'd received a permit starting July 9, 2023, heading southbound from Hart's Pass in the heart of the Northern Cascades. Our vision was slowly becoming a reality.

2

Seems Crazy Not to Do It?

Permit in hand, our attention turned elsewhere. Throughout the winter of 2022/2023, I tracked snowfall totals at various points along the trail. Since the PCT passes through some of the United States' highest mountains, the snowpack is often late to melt out along the trail at these higher elevations. The trail winds past several volcanoes towering over 10,000 feet, such as mounts Baker, Adams, and Hood, and skirts the base of Mount Whitney, the highest mountain in the contiguous United States at 14,505 feet, highlighting the route's diverse and challenging terrain. With a baby in tow, we had selected a start date that fell after the average historical meltout, making it our goal to be hiking on dirt, even in alpine terrain. I followed the SNOTEL weather stations in Washington and Oregon most intently since we would have to pass through those areas first. Snow fell throughout the winter, but at a rate and depth slightly lower than normal. By mid-March, it appeared that the season's total had reached its peak. Barring any further snowstorms or a cold spring, we stood a good chance of enjoying a snow-free hike through the Cascades.

Meanwhile, farther south, the Sierras were experiencing their largest snowfall in decades. Snow fell continuously throughout the winter, resulting in a seasonal snowpack 300 percent above the historical norm, with places like Mammoth Lakes, California, receiving 92 feet of snow over the winter. Continued snowfall into spring all but guaranteed a lingering snowpack deep into the summer for anyone on the trail.

Traditionally, nearly all thru-hikers (>90 percent) on the PCT start at the Mexican border, hiking north to Canada. This allows for a longer hiking season, permitting hikers to start in the desert in the spring and finish at the Canadian border in late fall. It also allows for a slower pace of travel. However, with the bulk of hikers starting at the same spot within a short period of time, there are often larger crowds on the trail, leading to what we believed would be less solitude or sense of wilderness. These large crowds often mean parties, which wasn't very appealing to us as thirty-something parents with an infant. Our interests lay elsewhere. We sought an immersive, wilderness like experience, leading us to decide to hike southbound instead, against the bulk of the traffic. While we would have a shorter time frame to get through the Sierras before the first major snowfall, which typically happens in October, heading south also offered us better overall weather, fewer bugs, and a better chance of avoiding lingering snow. If all went to plan, we'd be finishing up the trail in early December, our steady pace of twenty miles per day bringing us all the way to Mexico in just five months' time.

As the season began for northbound hikers—"NOBOs"—in late March and early April 2023, reports began to trickle in online about the substantial snow that remained in the Sierras. Hikers found themselves needing to use snowshoes, ice axes, and winter gear to advance each day. Many opted to hike at night when the snow surface was frozen, sleeping during the day when the sun turned the trail into slush. Vital bridges were destroyed in the rushing meltoff, forcing hikers to ford deep, fast, moving waters or detour for miles in other directions. Facebook PCT groups were abuzz with confusion, filled with hikers wondering about snow conditions and trying to determine their next steps.

When we told others—friends, family, strangers, you name it— about our plans, most of the responses were negative. For at least two thirds of those we told, the basic response was a scrunched-up face, followed by, "And you're going to do this with the baby?" Everyone seemed to have some type of opinion, and each wanted to weigh in. My dad, skeptical of our plans, remarked that he'd see us in August, though our projected end date was in early December. My mom, always the worrier, continually asked throughout the planning process why we were doing this, wondering why we didn't wait until Enedina was older or simply choose a shorter trip. The receptionist at our pediatrician's office sarcastically commented that it would be "a ton of fun." And still others simply suggested that it was not possible, due to the long distances, heavy packs, and any number of other factors related to dealing with a baby on a thru-hike.

We weren't opposed to hearing criticism, but much of the feedback seemed more like knee-jerk reactions that reflected each naysayer's capabilities or interests, rather than our own. Anyone who has raised children knows well the experience of being on the receiving end of parenting advice, often unsolicited. Throw in something novel for the twenty-first century, like living outside in a tent for five months, and you open a can of worms.

Ironically, if we stayed home and parked our daughter in front of an iPad for multiple hours a day, most people wouldn't have batted an eye, even though screen time has been widely shown to lead to the degradation of eyesight, coordination, and general development in babies and children. Yet head outside with clean air, water, and a natural environment that is a known boon to childhood development and adult well-being, and suddenly you're the "crazy" one.

While there was skepticism, we also received encouragement and support. Those in our corner prodded us on, asking if we needed help with preparations and offering assistance for whatever might come up while we were on the trail. My friend Cody, himself an avid outdoorsman and accomplished trail runner, bolstered our confidence by reframing our trip in the modern context:

> "You mean, you're going to make a journey similar to many of our human ancestors (who also had baby in tow), but with all of the safety nets of your wilderness competence using modern equipment, wilderness skills honed in an objectively harsher environment, modern communication technology, modern medicine, food resources, and general societal infrastructure on a well-trodden route with many other hikers and the option to bail at basically any point?
>
> Seems crazy NOT to do it, in my opinion."

To check all of our bases, we met with Enedina's pediatrician to see what advice she had regarding the trip and whether there was anything special we should bring. She didn't discourage us in the slightest, only telling us to be careful with insects and check the CDC guidelines for viruses in the areas we'd be hiking through. We weren't worried about damaging Din's development by undertaking this trip, nor, with our skills and experience, did we fear being unprepared for what could happen on the trail. We both have extensive medical training, having taken multiple wilderness first aid and wilderness first responder courses, and at one point we were both certified Emergency Medical Technicians (EMTs). Meanwhile, our experience camping with Din in the Southwest, during which we had spent our days hiking up to twelve miles off-trail into remote side canyons in the sandstone desert, had come off without a hitch.

Reviewing the literature, we didn't find anything that would suggest the trip would be a foolhardy endeavor either. The widely proclaimed "bible of wilderness medicine," *Auerbach's Wilderness Medicine*, has an entire chapter devoted to travel with infants and spending time with children in the wilderness. The main points of consideration for infants are thermoregulation, diaper rash, and fluid retention in the event of an intestinal illness. Without Enedina having any pre-existing conditions to worry about, we felt confident that we could go forth on the trail without risking her well-being. If anything came up, neither of us were so headstrong that we wouldn't reevaluate our options and consider leaving the trail altogether.

The quote by the renowned philosopher Jiddu Krishnamurti, "It's no measure of health to be well adjusted to a profoundly sick society," often came to mind throughout our preparations. The societal norms we observed intuitively seemed wrong, and we had no interest in following them. These norms have had serious consequences, leading to a decline in children's physical and mental health. For instance, nearly 20 percent of kids in the United States classify as obese,[1] an alarming statistic made even more troubling when you consider that roughly the same percentage of children regularly take some type of prescription

1. According to data from 2020 from the Center for Disease Control. A number that has likely grown higher following the pandemic, which intensified earlier trends of time spent indoors, time on screens, and sedentary behavior. Source: https://www.cdc.gov/obesity/data/childhood.html

drug for psychiatric issues.[2] These aren't signs of a healthy society, and served as examples that we actively sought to avoid. From our vantage point, it wasn't difficult to see how such problems came about.

Richard Louv, in his pivotal book *The Last Child in the Woods,* discusses the various trends and challenges shaping the younger generations: "...a severance of the public and private mind from our food's origins; a disappearing line between machines, humans and other animals; an increasingly intellectual understanding of our relationship with other animals; the invasion of our cities by wild animals (even as urban/suburban designers replace wildness with synthetic nature); and the rise of a new kind of suburban form." In modern times, most kids rarely leave the house, leading lives largely devoid of risk or consequence amidst plastic toys and padded surfaces. Louv highlights the phenomenon of "containerized kids" in an early chapter:

> "Jane Clark, a University of Maryland professor of kinesiology (the study of human movement), calls them 'containerized kids'—they spend more and more time in car seats, high chairs, and even baby seats for watching TV. When small children do go outside, they're often placed in containers—strollers—and pushed by walking or jogging parents. Most kid-containerizing is done for

---

2. Source: https://www.cchrint.org/psychiatric-drugs/children-on-psychiatric-drugs/

safety concerns, but the long-term health of these children is compromised."[3]

Louv goes on to discuss a study from researchers at the University of Glasgow, Scotland that tracked toddler activity for a week, finding that a group of three-year-olds was only physically active for twenty minutes a day. Studies elsewhere came to similar conclusions, suggesting that the separation from nature is part of a broader trend toward more restrictive lifestyles for children. Written in 2008, Louv's book addresses the trends in a world that hadn't yet been fully overwhelmed by digital devices. Today, kids' independence is even more limited, with screen time ever more prevalent at home and school, leading to a disconnection from their local environment—which results in most kids knowing more corporations by age 5 than native plants in their backyard. Louv notes, "A kid today can likely tell you about the Amazon rain forest but not about the last time he or she explored the woods in solitude, or lay in a field listening to the wind and watching the clouds move." To us this raised the question: *Which was the aberration? Our lifestyle? Or the "new" ways of doing things?*

With Din, Alana and I aimed to create an environment that stood in opposition to the societal norm. We envisioned a setting in which she could explore, understand, and engage with the natural world, free from an overload of artificial stimulation. We sought an upbringing that nurtured her creativity, encouraging her to invent her own games and find joy, without dependence on specific items. Moreover, we wanted her childhood to

---

3. Louv, Richard. *The Last Child in the Woods.* 2008, p. 28. Kindle.

be one in which she felt confident taking risks, using her physical and mental abilities to tackle challenges and develop skills.

Our home in Fairbanks reflects that desire, offering us daily interactions with the natural world. Positioned in the forest, our yard alone presents numerous opportunities for challenge and engagement with nature. We live less than 10 miles from the nearest grizzly track and are even closer to areas frequented by wolves—we live on the doorstep of a vast ecosystem brimming with opportunities for learning, living, and exploration. These daily encounters have ingrained these beliefs into our lifestyle, necessitating constant involvement by design; it's a life we feel blessed to share with Din.

Alana, who spent most of her twenties living in a tent, grew accustomed to a lifestyle far different from most. Her work on trail crews took her to remote reaches of the West and Alaska. There, after hiking in with chainsaws, hand tools, days' worth of water and food, and camping gear, she would live and work for weeks at a time. These experiences not only made her comfortable living and being in wilderness environments for long stretches but also toughened her against the elements and the inherent challenges that go with the outdoor lifestyle. She leveraged these hard-earned skills to build the life she wanted in Alaska, working on remote sections of trail in the summer and snowboarding down its mountains in the darkness and deep cold of winter.

Independently, I had been introduced to much of the same mentality and skills through my NOLS course, spending 75 days sea kayaking, backpacking, and glacial mountaineering in some of Alaska's most rugged environments. At age 20, this experience was transformative, cementing my love for the state and leading me to move from the Lower 48 to the Arctic not long thereafter. I cut my teeth in the Brooks Range, learning how to travel in big wilderness by foot, raft, and ski. With only about 30 people living on the road system in the Central Brooks Range, I felt as if the mountains were my personal playground, and I took every opportunity to go deeper, travel more efficiently, and learn to read the land. Inspired by the traditional lifestyle of old, I tried my hand at living a subsistence lifestyle, based out of a 1930s 12'x12' miner's cabin in the village of Wiseman, population 13. I taught myself how to hunt and fish, heated my cabin with wood, hauled water from the river, and relied on a small solar panel for power. Living off grid and 240 miles from the nearest town or services, the learning curve was steep, and any mistakes were magnified. But as the years went by, my experience and knowledge grew to the extent that I was not only comfortable hiking on my own in the mountains for a day but heading out on remote trips dozens of miles from the nearest town or village for days at a time alone.

A sense of loneliness eventually brought me south to Fairbanks, where in 2018 I started working for the state's forest-inventory program, measuring trees and vegetation. That's where I met Alana. After nearly a decade of being single, I had just about given up on finding a companion within the state's frozen expanses. While many people have traveled north to Alaska seeking worldly treasure like furs, whales, gold, and oil, only the truly foolish come here in search of companionship. The cold and darkness do a lot to dissuade many from coming or staying, and the population reflects that, with the state holding the title of America's highest male-to-female ratio.[4] At the end of the road, there is no shortage of characters, leading to the saying for women trying to find a man here that "The odds are good, but the goods are odd."

Alana and I were assigned to the same shift during my third year in forestry—2020—and it was then that our relationship

---

4. At 109 men for every 100 women.

blossomed. The program operated out of sparsely populated, remote outposts within the state. Each day, we'd get dropped off early in an even more remote locale off the road system, hiking to predetermined coordinates where we'd perform our measurements, counting and assessing trees, documenting the vegetation within each area, and taking soil samples, before returning to base. The job involved exposure to all kinds of risks, from helicopter travel to hypothermia to wild animals. Alana had experienced more of those risks than most, once having even had a close encounter with a charging grizzly bear that stopped within mere feet of her.

Early in that summer's training, Alana and I became inseparable. Throughout that summer, we'd look to spend any free moment together, passing evenings by swimming in lakes, paddleboarding, or canoeing out to secluded coves. I was taken in by her playfulness, which often turned otherwise-mundane moments, like waiting in a construction zone on the highway, into something memorable, like a pistachio-shell fight. When we were on the same crew during the day, we'd joke around, share stories about our pasts and learn more about each other. Some nights, we'd go up high in the mountains, searching for signs of early blueberries. We usually only found remnant snow from the previous winter, which Alana made sure to share with me as a barrage of snowballs. That summer, I began building what is now our home, and Alana was there the very first day to help me lay out the foundation, frequently returning later to lend a hand. During one of our breaks from work, we took a hiking and packrafting trip to Alaska's Forty Mile Mountains. At Alana's insistence, we'd wrestle at night[5] and dance salsa on barren ridge tops by day. Days into our trip, with the land as our

---

5. No that's not a euphemism—we actually wrestled.

sole company, we confessed our feelings for each other, and our romantic relationship was born.

We used that summer as a launching pad to build the life we wanted, a life centered on spending as much time as possible with each other and in the outdoors. From our base in Fairbanks, we went all over the state, skiing dozens of miles to remote cabins, walking along the shores of tumultuous rivers in search of salmon, trekking over hillsides in search of caribou, and floating past countless moose on glacier-fed rivers. We'd bask in the endless sun of summer and cuddle close next to the wood stove during the frigid nights of winter. With little body fat and my propensity for getting wet from rain, rivers, or a combination of both, there was many a time when Alana had come to my rescue, getting me warmed up and out of hypothermia. As our relationship developed, so did our trips, with us staying out longer and going farther afield. In 2021, we participated in the state's most arduous wilderness race, the Alaska Mountain Wilderness Classic, packrafting and trekking off-trail, covering about 100 miles, self-supported through a portion of the rugged Talkeetna Mountains.

After we finished building our home in early 2021, Alana found joy in developing our large garden and in operating her business, teaching the chainsaw skills she'd learned on her trail-crew days to other women. After years of traveling around and working seasonally, she was content to finally settle down and establish deeper roots. She had grown into the exemplar of an All-Alaskan Woman: skilled in baking, hunting, traversing rough terrain, and enduring the elements and insects, all while maintaining a sense of humor. "It's just water— what's the big deal," she'd say, challenging my reluctance to hike or ski in bad weather, and then add, "We're adults. We make the rules." Her spirited independence and readiness to act without seeking others' approval led to a life in which our possibilities seemed boundless. It was hard to believe that I'd not only been able to find someone who shared my values, but challenged me to be stronger, better, and tougher along the way. I couldn't imagine life without her.

Taking five months off work without being paid to hike the PCT is something that stretches the imagination for most working adults, let alone adults with children. We had someone ask us if we were trust-fund kids and others who were incredulous that we were able to carve out so much free time. But the reality was far less romantic. Alana and I had decided when we began dating that we would prioritize the things in life that were most important to us, letting the rest of our lives fall in line to support this vision. We live simply, residing in a 320-square-foot home that we built ourselves, sourcing as much of our own food as we can by hunting and fishing in the Alaskan backcountry, cooking nearly all our meals at home, and eschewing the trappings of material goods. Our simple and frugal lifestyle means that saving money becomes easy no matter what paid work we do, allowing for a lot more optionality and freedom when desired.

After years of living this way, we had accumulated substantial savings—enough to live without paid work for several years, what some might call "fuck-you money." Alana had in fact stopped working shortly before Din was born, leaving me as the only working stiff in the family. In the winter of 2018, I started working remotely and on a seasonal basis for my dad, in his insurance business. As my relationship with Alana developed, the thought of spending more time away from her working forestry grew less and less appealing, prompting me to shelve forestry work and begin working for my dad full-time in late 2020. Although I had stable employment through the family business, I was uncertain about how my decision to hike the PCT would be received by my father. My plan was to explain our intentions to him regarding our trip, expressing my desire to return to work post-hike, but also being prepared to move on if that was not an option.

Despite our financial stability, the thought of initiating this conversation made me nervous. By going on the PCT, I would potentially forego the "security" that comes with a stable job, but in its stead would be a sense of freedom, time with my family, and a once-in-a-lifetime opportunity. In my head, I went through countless simulations of the conversation. As the months passed, the time to have the discussion with my father finally arrived, and it unfolded somewhat like this:

"Alana and I are going to hike the Pacific Crest Trail starting in July."
"How long will you be gone?"
"About five months."
"So you probably won't have service anywhere on the trail?"
"No, not really. We'll have some access in the towns we pass through along the way. I could maybe do some work there every few days."
"Oh yeah—you won't want to do that then. Okay—we'll have to find someone to do your stuff until you come back."

There was nothing to be worried about after all. With work taken care of, all our dominoes were falling into place. Barring injury or illness, nothing stood in the way of us undertaking the trip.

3

Getting Ready

In early February of 2023, we dove into our preparations for the trip, many of which were uniquely tailored to life on the trail with an infant. We faced the reality that we needed to take care of not just ourselves, but also Din. *Would we not only be able to do this, but also enjoy ourselves?* we wondered.

Throughout our adult lives, Alana and I have taken joy in living simply and pursuing hard things, abiding by the mantra "Easy choices, hard life. Hard choices, easy life." Our lives at home reflected that. Living off grid in a dry cabin requires us to do things like chop wood and carry water. By sourcing our own power and much of our own food, we put ourselves closer to the roots, gaining an understanding of the energy and resources our life requires. These self-imposed challenges bring us more contentment than the ease and convenience that modern society offers. We saw the trip and time on the PCT as an extension of that, an opportunity to have a more grounded and intensive experience, with minimal equipment.

Over the last twenty years, there has been an explosion in the popularity of backpacking and thru-hiking, fueled in part by ever-lighter gear. Historically, backpacking equipment was cumbersome, bulky, and heavy, and people brought a lot of it. Hiking was associated with hefty frame packs that towered well over people's heads and left hikers feeling haggard after each day of travel. There were some exceptions throughout history, like

John Muir, who was famous for hiking throughout the Sierras with just a tin cup and a stale loaf of bread. Another example was Ray Jardine, who along with his wife in the 1970s, started hiking all across the country, including trails like the PCT and Appalachian Trail, with lightweight gear they made themselves. Others began to catch on not long after, and eventually the gear companies did as well.

This led to somewhat of a revolution in hiking styles. Boots were replaced with lightweight trail runners. Bulky sleeping bags were switched out for quilts, while many superfluous items like camp chairs, big stoves, lanterns, and large cookware were left at home. These changes allowed hikers to push the limits, going with smaller packs and traveling longer distances with ease. Ultralight hiking, defined by carrying a base weight[1] of twenty pounds or less, became a goal for many. This is a significant reduction compared to that of the traditional backpacker, who lugs around a pack with a base weight hovering around thirty-five pounds. There was even the creation of the "super ultralight" category, for a base weight of less than ten pounds. This mindset brought about sayings like "Every ounce counts," as well as ridiculous practices like people cutting off the end of their toothbrush to reduce weight.

The change in mindset and gear allowed hikers to go farther and faster. Normal days of ten to fifteen trail miles jumped to a new standard of twenty-five miles or more. Some people, like the famed hiker Andrew Skurka, took this farther-and-faster mindset to the limit, hiking thirty miles a day every day to connect multiple trails within one season. Others would use the techniques to go after speed records, blazing through long trails within a couple of months, instead of taking up to half a year.

---

1. Pack weight minus food and water.

Roman Dial, one of Alaska's most accomplished adventurers, created a rough heuristic for walking distance relative to weight. In 2006, he walked over 600 miles in 26 days across the northern Brooks Range, completely self-contained and unsupported. That effort forced him to consider what items were essential, how to travel efficiently, and what was reasonable in terms of daily distance traveled. His idea was that each additional pound added to your pack decreases the maximum distance you can cover in a day by one mile. So, for example, if the maximum distance you could walk in a day is 70 miles, a 50-pound pack would reduce your maximum distance to 20 miles. It isn't perfect, as someone fit enough to hike 70 miles a day could realistically carry a 75-pound pack at least one mile, but it is useful in terms of gauging what is possible and what is Herculean.

While considering our own trip, we looked at the average weight of a one-year-old baby. Most literature suggested around twenty pounds for girls, a manageable weight. Since she was not yet a year old, we figured Din would likely weigh a little less than that early on while we got our legs underneath us, and then slightly more toward the end of the trail. We'd be carrying far more than almost every other thru-hiker on the PCT, but in our minds, this remained within the realm of possibility.

Not long after Din was born, my stepmom gifted us the best baby carrier on the market at the time, the Osprey Poco Plus, essentially a backpack with a harnessed seat that faced the wearer's head, which would give us the ability to carry Din. The Poco Plus also had an additional twenty-six liters of storage space (equivalent to a larger day pack), but it weighed eight pounds when completely empty. This meant that if Din was average weight, the lowest base weight that pack would ever be was twenty-eight pounds. Yikes.

With this twenty-eight extra pounds in mind, we had to be ruthless about what we brought. Anything that could not be justified wouldn't make it on the trip. For sleeping pads, we opt-ed for closed-cell-foam pads in lieu of comfier inflatable ones. We decided to sew a double quilt for all three of us, rather than carrying our individual sleeping bags, which would be heavier and take up more space. Books, extra clothes, individual pots and bowls, baby bottles, toys, camp shoes? No way. All that would stay at home.

Alana took the lead in sorting gear, while I focused on the lo-gistics, creating spreadsheets that outlined our resupply strategy and food plan. She meticulously went through our equipment, sorting it to determine what we could use and what we needed to source elsewhere. After organizing everything into piles, she rifled through them, further sorting again. On top of that, she learned how to sew over the course of three weeks, spending a few evenings after Din had gone to bed crafting a silver 35-de-gree sleeping quilt.

While our work in forestry and lives in Alaska had gotten us accustomed to wearing heavy packs—lugging gear for measur-ing trees and packing out meat and fish after getting lucky on hunting and fishing excursions—none of those times involved hiking eighteen to twenty miles a day, let alone for five months straight. This was going to be a unique challenge! We decided that Alana would carry Din in the carrier, along with a few lighter things like toiletries, and I would carry everything else in the other pack. Our goal was to each carry a total pack weight averaging thirty and thirty-five pounds respectively.

We were well prepared in another sense, in that we didn't have to buy much gear—years of backpacking and camping had left us mostly outfitted. That bolstered our confidence because we knew how to use what we had and how it would perform in rough conditions. We also knew the myriad ways in which our gear could fail and could prepare for that as well.

However, the same couldn't be said for baby gear for Din. As far as we could tell, any gear options were targeted toward the larger market: families going out on short day hikes who weren't concerned with weight and weren't carrying multiple days' worth of supplies.

We had used the carrier extensively, so we knew that Din was comfortable in it for at least a couple hours at a time. She was still primarily breastfeeding and would continue to do so while we were on the trail, supplemented with some of our own food. Eating had never been a problem for her. Sleeping, on the other hand, was a different story. In the nine months since she was born, she had not slept through the night once. The most common pattern was that she'd awake two to three times a night, and then Alana would feed her back to sleep. On the worst nights, she would be up at least every hour, consoled only by nursing. She also co-slept with us in our bed, which often resulted in a lot of frustration and exhaustion on our end.

Our biggest uncertainty lay around diapers: Would we be able to carry enough if we brought disposables? And if we brought cloth diapers, would we be able to wash them? I took to the internet to see if anyone had gone for long distances with a baby and how they dealt with this situation. All I found was the couple who had hiked part of the Appalachian Trail and used compostable diapers. There was an idea—we could get compostables and bury or burn them along the way! But a search of the worldwide marketplace didn't yield any viable results. On further thought, I was also hard pressed to believe that diapers would compost in a reasonable time period and didn't feel comfortable burying or burning them. We'd have to look elsewhere.

Reusable cloth diapers started to seem like the best option. We had used them since Din was born without issue and we were accustomed to washing them with a minimal water supply, so any adjustment to washing on the trail would be miniscule. The climate along the PCT is arid, so it seemed feasible to hang the cloth inserts (which comprise the bulk of the absorbent layer) and the outer covers to dry at camp or on the pack. Alana had looked far and wide to find sets that were quick drying, while still absorbent, testing each one at home. To make things simpler, we opted to include a day's worth of disposable diapers for each resupply as well. That way, if we couldn't wash the cloth diapers due to lack of water, dry them due to rain, or needed something around town, we would have an alternative.

With the big questions around Din out of the way, we moved on to figuring out the details of our own food and gear. On most of the trail, options for resupply would be limited to small local grocers or convenience stores—options that were very limited, expensive, and likely not nutritionally adequate. So we decided to make our own food for the bulk of the trip, preparing boxes to be shipped to us along the way and planning to shop locally in towns where there were larger grocers. We dehydrated beans and lentils, roasted nuts, made granola, and mixed ingredients together. We hoped to catch some salmon and make jerky for snacks, but with a slow run and no sign of increase by late June, that didn't seem a viable option. Somewhat reluctantly due to the cost, we opted for store-bought beef jerky instead.

Throughout our preparations, we trained as much as we could. Alana and I aren't strangers to exercise, but we wanted to ensure we were in the best shape possible for the trail. We took to our kettlebells, the pool, and our Airdyne fan bike. Additionally, a few times a week, we'd load up our packs with over forty pounds, including Din and weighted plates, to explore local trails or go up Moose Mountain, the nearby ski hill.

Early on, we were able to stick to our schedule of training five days a week. But as the weeks went on and our sleep quality did not improve, it became harder and harder for us to muster any energy. It didn't seem smart to train exhausted when we knew we weren't going to get any rest later, so naps were often substituted in training's stead.

Despite this, Alana, who was likely more tired from dealing with nursing throughout the day as well as the sleepless nights, was usually the one to prod us on, insisting we stick to our schedule, whether it involved climbing the hill, cycling, or swimming. In her mind, we weren't doing enough.

"It'll be fine." I reassured her. "There's a trail. It can't be that hard."

4

An Uneven Path

While each of us had our own worries about the trail and how Din would fare, there would be other challenges along the way. In particular, interpersonal challenges. Our marriage would be tested to the limit, strained under the stress of a newborn baby, life on the trail, and the physical and mental exhaustion that comes with both. Adversity and uncertainty in our relationship were nothing new to us. Alana and I had already put our relationship through various stressors— building our house, competing in that Alaskan wilderness race together, traveling abroad—but despite all this, had strayed very little from our initial joyous infatuation with each other.

At home, as we got ready for the PCT, we continued to joke, act silly, and wrestle. I'd frequently find myself having to fend off Alana's tickle attacks. Other times I'd open my laptop, unfold clothes, or go to the kitchen only to find a love note waiting for me. A friend of ours had told us that he loved getting married because he felt that it gave his wife and him permission to be even sillier than before. That seemed to be no different in our case. One of Alana's sisters had repeatedly told us that we seemed made for each other. Often our relationship felt like a fairy tale, with everything humming along perfectly.

Yet, like all couples, we had our ups and downs. There were times when everything flowed smoothly and times when we struggled to get our points across to each other. Much of this was compounded by the fact that we spend a good chunk of time together, within the confines of our tiny home. My parents' divorce when I was 12 had left a lasting impact, and I was determined not to follow in their footsteps. In an effort to be different, I had focused on improving my communication skills, searching for insight within various self-help books like *How to Have Impossible Conversations* and *Mistakes Were Made (But Not by Me)*.

But as I was to discover, there is a big difference between knowing a thing and executing it well. Throughout my life, I've battled my ego, which has often tried to control my actions and decisions; when my ego rears its ugly head, I usually become overbearing, taking control of projects and insisting on doing things my way. I have my own theories on where this may have originated, but who knows its true origins. I figure it likely began during my parents' messy divorce and the extensive bullying I endured at school during the same period. At the time, I came up with a defensive mechanism—taking control, avoiding conflict, and shutting down—to forge on through those rough moments. But when they ended, I subconsciously kept my walls up and defenses in place, a pattern that has, at times, left me counterproductively hurting others instead of helping them. Alana was patient with me at first, but rightfully became increasingly frustrated as time wore on and she felt unheard in our relationship. The learning process was long, and the implementation process even longer.

Despite my efforts to improve our dynamic, old patterns resurfaced in our planning process, leading us to wonder at certain moments if the trail was even worth it. Days before leaving, with both of us anxious about our departure and tired from the months of preparation, a disagreement over how to pack our resupply boxes escalated into a larger argument, resulting in hours of silence, less than forty-eight hours before our flight south. With boxes and gear strewn throughout every inch of our tiny home, Din busily transferring food from one box to another, and a list of chores yet to be done, I decided to finally address the issue.

"Are we going to talk about this?" I asked.
"What's the point? You don't listen. We should just not go."
"What?! Why?"
"We're not even talking now. And we're going to go spend five months in even closer proximity to each other?"
"We've worked months planning for this trip. It seems silly to throw it all away over something like this. It's not anything we can't work past."

Since Din's birth, the ease of our communication had slowly begun to diminish, strained by months of sleepless nights, withering patience, and endless tasks. We were still figuring it all out, and the additional stress of planning and preparing for the PCT certainly wasn't helping matters. Meanwhile, Alana was grappling on her own with becoming a mother and its responsibilities, finding nearly all her free time and thoughts consumed by caring for our daughter. After another half hour of conversation, we managed to patch things up temporarily, duct-taping the leaks in our communication. We would go forth with our plans after all, but without any change in the underlying circumstances of our relationship, this temporary fix could only last so long.

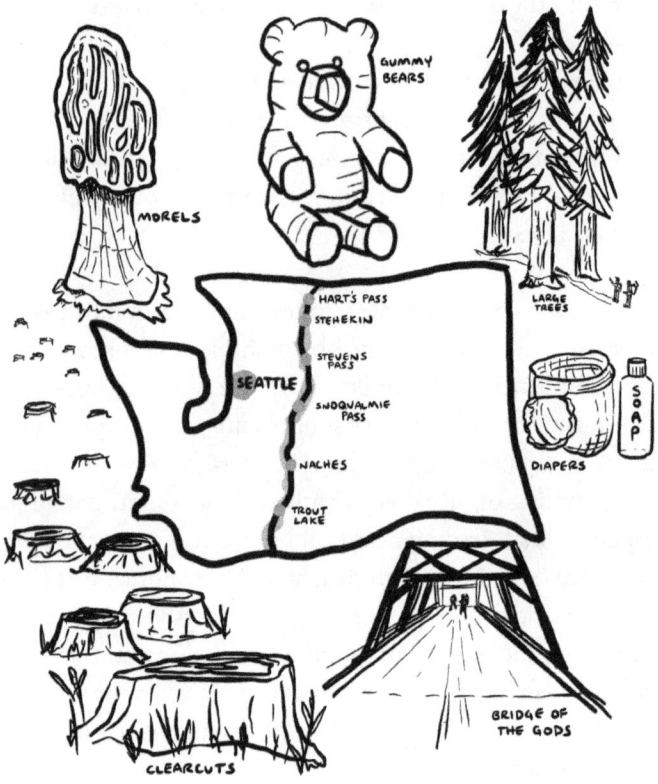

MORELS

GUMMY BEARS

LARGE TREES

HART'S PASS
STEHEKIN
STEVENS PASS
SEATTLE
SNOQUALMIE PASS
NACHES
TROUT LAKE

SOAP

DIAPERS

CLEARCUTS

BRIDGE OF THE GODS

WASHINGTON

5

The Start

Hart's Pass, Washington

"Is that baby going to Mexico?"

After traveling for over twenty-four hours, we had finally arrived at our launching point. Planes had brought us from our home in Fairbanks to Wenatchee, Washington, from where we took a series of progressively smaller buses and shuttles farther north to Hart's Pass. Thirty miles south of the Canadian border, Hart's Pass (6,204 feet) is the PCT's northernmost access point. A 30-mile jaunt to the north would bring one to a series of wooden posts, marking the northern terminus of the trail. Most thru-hikers opt to finish or start at the border, but we weren't interested in trekking the extra 60 miles to reach the border and come back. Our trip was bound to be challenging enough as it was, especially since Enedina, now 9 months old, weighed a solid 21 pounds.

Nestled near treeline atop the pass, surrounded by mountains, some tents and cars dotted the campground. As we organized our packs and readied to hit the trail, we overheard other hikers talking about us and casting curious glances our way.

"I wonder what they're doing about food."
"Are you sure they're thru-hiking with that baby?"

Alana found the trail register and made an entry:
Date: 7/8/23
Name: The McClures
From: Alaska
Direction: SOBO

It was just after 6 p.m., but we didn't have much interest in sticking around, pitching a tent among the dozen others in the campground and starting in the morning. The midsummer sun still hung well above the horizon, and with no signs of twilight, we embarked on our journey to Mexico. You would think that such a moment would be momentous, that we'd pass a marker or sign that proclaimed "You are now hiking the PCT!" and we'd feel like we're finally doing it, off on our grand journey! But no. Seconds in, we got momentarily lost, confused by multiple pathways and the lack of signage. We couldn't find the trail. Like nearly everyone else, we were using FarOut, a mobile mapping app for navigation. In our preparations for the trip, I had asked Alana, "What do we do if our phones run out of battery?" She had responded saying, "The trail is really well marked, it'd be really hard to get lost." Now here we were, not even a mile into the trek, hell, not even out of the parking lot, stumbling around in circles. Bashfully, I pulled my phone out of my pocket, checked the GPS, and found the trail. Moments later, we were en route, bounding away up a hill. Southward ho!

Alpine wildflowers, such as Tuolumne and Indian paintbrush, lined the trail, with blueberry bushes just beyond, still months from fruiting. Enedina was content in her perch atop the baby carrier, babbling away at the trees and flowers. To the west, mountains extended as far as the horizon and a dense, forested, unpeopled valley lay below. Our destination for the night, only six miles away, approached quickly with our fresh legs. We soon found our campsite: an open, flat, compacted area in the trees just off the trail. A creek bubbled just downhill, and we spotted another tent through the trees about fifty yards away.

At camp, as I waited for water to heat up for some dehydrated rice and beans, I decided to dip into one of our homemade snack mixes, a concoction named "raw cookie dough" that consisted of crushed cashews, maple syrup, peanut butter, and vanilla. It was one of our favorites of everything that we'd packed, but as the first bites hit my mouth, I could tell something was off. I didn't taste the sweetness of the syrup or the savoriness of the nuts. Instead, the snack mix tasted almost chemical.

"Did you use this bag for our laundry detergent?" I asked Alana.

"No, that's all in one bag at home."

"Ugh—this tastes like soap."

"That's weird. We don't even have any of the laundry detergent with us."

How could it taste like soap? These were brand-new bags and we had, in our rigorous preparations, sampled everything at home with no ill results. Then it dawned on us. The "all-natural" insect- repellent wipes we'd packed to protect our baby from mosquitoes were in a plastic bag next to our food. The citronella and essential oils from the wipes had somehow permeated through both bags, contaminating the food. Just hours into our trip, our supply had already been compromised. Fortunately, our dinner wasn't affected, but we now had several pounds of citronella-tainted food in our packs. *Strike one.*

As we ate, mosquitoes buzzed around, and we swatted them away lazily. We had already gone through Alaska's mosquito season, when you can sometimes measure the density of mosquitoes by how many you can kill with one hand. Earlier in the summer, a friend was hiking in Denali National Park and counted nearly 100 dead with one swat. So, while we'd heard and read reports from other hikers about hordes of mosquitoes in Washington and Oregon, as seasoned Alaskans, we weren't too concerned. In fact, thanks to my overconfidence, we had left our tent's inner bug net at home, bringing only head nets.

Exhausted from the long day of travel, we turned in early. Din fell asleep quickly, but not long after, the sound of something walking near our food cache startled us. A bear on the first night? It sounded like it was continuing toward our tent. I grabbed my headlamp and shined the light out from under the edge of our mid, a tipi like tent with no floor, open all along the bottom edge. The light shone on a deer, feeding contentedly off whatever sparse scraps we had dropped in the dirt. It looked up at the light and bounded off.

Relieved that there wasn't a bear tromping around camp, I tried to go back to sleep. I stared up at the green nylon of the tent, too jazzed for rest. Minutes later, I heard more movement—this time in and around the tent and of a more muted nature, something scurrying. *What the hell?* I grabbed the light once more after something touched my head. Mice! I banged my hands on the ground and pack hoping to scare them off, inadvertently waking Alana and Din. Meanwhile, the mosquitoes had continued to build, infiltrating our tent under the open sides. They weren't thick, but their incessant whining and landing on our faces every few minutes was enough to keep us from sleeping. By the end of our first hour at attempted sleep, Din had woken intermittently screaming, inconsolable. Alana and I argued about what to do, finding no solution. Din would wake repeatedly throughout the night, overtired and comforted only by feeding, leaving Alana frustrated and in tears.

Collectively, Alana and I managed maybe three hours of sleep, what Alana—annoyed that I hadn't brought the tent's bug net—called her "worst night of sleep ever." *Strike two.*

As temperatures cooled, the mosquitoes died down and eventually the sun rose, greeting us with a new day, our first full one on the trail. Bleary-eyed, we sheepishly greeted the people from the nearby tent and apologized for all the commotion as we packed up to leave. Before setting off, Alana was going to grab some water from the nearby creek and wash Din's diapers from the day before.

"Can you get me the soap from your bag?" Alana asked.

"No, it's in your bag."

"No, it's not."

"Yes, it is—I'll get it."

A check of her pack, then my pack, and then both packs again indeed proved that she did not have the soap. And neither did I. We'd managed to forget perhaps the key item that would make our diaper-cleaning strategy work. *Strike three.*

Doubts and negative thoughts raced through our minds. How were we going to walk 2,600 miles with a baby if we couldn't even make it one night without descending into chaos? Were we foolish for attempting this? What the hell were we thinking?

6

The North Cascades

Hart's Pass to Stehekin, Washington
July 8–July 11 50 miles

Initially, the social aspect of the trail was as we had expected. Over the course of the first few days, we encountered about ten to twenty people, leaving us with hours of time and miles to ourselves. Usually, we exchanged greetings with those we overtook or met coming in the opposite direction, talking only for a moment or two before continuing on. Other times we'd step off the trail, trading stories and information about the route ahead with the other hikers. Surprise often greeted the littlest member of our group, and one passerby even mistook the contents atop Alana's baby carrier for a dog. Despite the lack of abundant interactions, two notable incidents stood out.

Our gaze while walking was often cast slightly downward and forward, scoping out the path ahead and navigating around rocks and roots. On the second day, we started noticing bright, colorful gummy bears lying in the trail—we assumed someone had accidentally dropped them while snacking on the go. But then we'd find another bear about a mile later, and another not long after that. We made it our mission to find the culprit, judging each person that we passed and evaluating whether they would be the type to eat gummy bears *and* lose a few along the way. We were the gummy-bear detectives, steadfast in our efforts to solve the case.

On day three, after taking in the panoramic views of the rugged mountains, we began descending from Cutthroat Pass and stopped at a small creek to filter water and fill up our bottles while Din was sleeping in the pack. A small side trail led off to some campsites just past the creek, back in the woods. But just before the trail curved out of sight, we spied something lying there orange and oddly shaped, out of place among the nearby shrubs and trees. Alana went to investigate and picked up what turned out to be a small orange ditty bag. She opened it, looked inside, and her jaw dropped. Lo and behold, inside was nothing other than a small, half-eaten package of gummy bears. What was happening here? Was someone trying to signal others? Were they trying to signal us? Or was this just a classic case of someone who was incredibly incompetent at snacking? The trail went cold after this last score, and to this day, the case remains unsolved.

After getting tormented by mosquitoes the first two nights of the trail, Din's face was looking a little worse for the wear, with bites spread across her cheeks. We worried about bugs from then on, making a point to find drier and windier areas to camp. Despite the bites, her demeanor remained unaffected, and she'd happily play with sticks during breaks and enjoy her time in the pack checking out new vistas. This came as a relief to Alana and me, as we were still getting our bearings, trying to figure out a good schedule that balanced making miles with taking care of Din. Early on, that balance was heavily weighted toward Din. Unable to get her to nap in the pack consistently, we took to taking long midday breaks, stretching out a sleeping pad off the trail beneath the trees so that she could sleep.

A day after our gummy-bear mystery, we entered North Cascades National Park. Soon thereafter, we stopped at a log to give

Din a chance to nap outside the pack. Not long after we got back on trail, the sky opened up and it began to pour. Donning our rain jackets, we continued on, anxious to get as close as we could to the town of Stehekin by sunset in order to set us up for a quick resupply the next day. While we fought our way through a thicket of alders, cow parsnip, and devil's club, we were greeted by an oncoming hiker with an outsized red pack.

"Good afternoon. I'm Aaron, a backcountry ranger with North Cascades National Park. Where are you guys heading today?"

"Bridger Campground, I think. It's by the road."

"There is no campground with that name."

"I think it's about five miles from the bus pickup to Stehekin," I answered.

The ranger eyed me suspiciously, and then asked to see our permits, required for anyone camping in the park. Rain continued to pour down, dripping off my hood and soaking everything that was exposed. Din sat in her perch behind me, silently looking on. Alana and I had swapped packs, so we fumbled around in the pockets, looking for each other's permits. She found mine first, and we passed it on to the ranger. After seeing that we were PCT thru-hikers and "true SOBOs" (southbound hikers), his manner completely changed. He apologized for stopping us and started treating us like royalty.

"Yes, there's the High Bridge Campground ten miles from here. It's about five miles from the road," he said.

By this time, I had found Alana's permit, but he waved it off, saying it was not necessary. He bid us luck and carried on, leaving us standing in the rain, rolling our eyes as he walked away.

The experience served as our introduction to the special treatment that thru-hikers occasionally enjoyed on the PCT, special treatment that often morphed into an expectation, creating a sense of entitlement and a holier-than-thou attitude among certain hikers we interacted with. Wearing their smugness on their sleeve like a badge, these thru-hikers belittled those who were out on shorter hikes, be it for a day, a week, or a section. To these hikers, the typical rules of the trail did not apply, a mindset that extended into towns as well, where it manifested in expecting discounts and extra benefits in stores and restaurants, often abandoning common courtesy and manners, as we would later discover.

Eventually the rain let up, and we continued farther into the forested valley beneath the mountains, making our way into the campground. There had been rumors of high bear activity in the area, enough to have me spooked come nightfall. But we had no unexpected visitors—only the sound of the rushing creek, a mere fifteen feet away, to keep us company. The only surprise of the evening was glancing above the maple canopy and being treated to a view of a clear night sky, blanketed with stars.

Our plan for the morning was to be on the trail by 7 a.m. to catch the 9 o'clock bus, one of two daily buses the National Park Service runs as a shuttle service for tourists and hikers. The trail would lead us five miles from the campground to the trailhead. From there, we'd reach one end of a ten-mile stretch of road to Stehekin, which is situated on the shores at one end of the fifty-mile-long Lake Chelan. We figured that if we caught the early bus, we'd have time to hang out in town, sort our resupply, and take the afternoon bus back to the trail later in the day, and then start hiking again. Missing either bus would mean that we'd have to find somewhere to stay or find another way to return to the trail before morning. With clear skies and warm weather, we were eager to take advantage of the conditions and make some miles.

I woke up first, fumbling around the quilt and the sleeping pads to find my phone to check the time: 7:10 a.m. I woke Alana and we set about packing everything quietly, leaving Din to sleep a little longer. By 7:35, Din was up, our tent and gear were packed, and we were away down the trail at our fastest pace yet. The terrain was relatively flat, allowing us to move quickly through the forest. Din was pleased throughout the first few miles, cooing and babbling along. Our early start coincided with other activity among the trees. I startled some mule deer that were bedded down, spooking them farther away from the trail. With two miles to go, Din was ready for her morning nap and starting to fuss, so I sang lullabies while racing on, sweat beading on my forehead. Checking the time frequently on my phone, I knew it would be close. We started to pass people whom we figured had taken the bus in, meaning if it hadn't already left yet, it would soon. We heard a horn honking, rounding a bend to see buildings coming into view. We sprinted down to the road and hopped on the blue bus with seconds to spare.

On the way into town, we stopped at the Stehekin Pastry Company, sampling their famous cinnamon roll and sticky bun[1] before continuing into town to grab our resupply boxes. At Lake Chelan in town, there were boats fastened to the dock, bobbing in the small chop, with sailboats moored farther offshore. We found a grassy spot near the water's edge in the sun. While Din slept in the grass, we got our packs in order, organizing our new food supply for the next five and a half days and gorging ourselves on leftover food from the previous section. We searched the town's two small stores, hoping to find some soap to wash Din's diapers with, but neither store offered what we were looking for, the closest thing being a bar of artisanal soap made from goat's milk. "Maybe we could just

---

1. #teamcinnamonroll

use that and rub really well?" I mused. Alana had other ideas and liberated a couple dozen pumps of foam hand soap from the public bathroom into a snack-sized Ziploc bag. Problem solved—for now.

Alana was smitten with the town and wanted to just settle down there. It was easy to see why: Stehekin had the quaint feel of an Alaskan town—remote, disconnected from the road, and with a culture of its own—but without the bugs. Before we caught the bus back, we walked about a mile and a half along the road, stopping to admire gardens and lakeside cabins, the finest of which had log dovetails without a thing out of place. Down the trail once more, we made camp after a few hours of walking. Our second section had begun.

7

Glacier Peak Wilderness

Stehekin to Stevens Pass, Washington
July 11–July 16 96 miles

From Stehekin, we walked into the Glacier Peak Wilderness, part of one of the longest sections of the PCT uninterrupted by roads or towns. This wilderness is also well known for its lack of maintenance. Each year, trees fall across the trail, while shrubs and other plants in the understory crowd up against its edges. Unchecked, the trail would eventually disappear, returning to the forest. As one of the country's most significant trails, the PCT receives regular maintenance by trail crews and volunteers, but this sixty-mile stretch through the wilderness area remains a notorious exception, and years of neglect have resulted in hundreds of downed trees lying across the trail. On the FarOut app, some people had made light of the situation, writing comments like:

"Welcome to the CrossFit Wilderness."

"Glacier Peak Wilderness hydration game. Take a sip of water every time there is a blowdown."

"Ah, the Glacier Peak Wilderness section of the PCT. I thought I signed up for a thru-hike, not *American Ninja Warrior.*"

Alana and I were no strangers to hiking over extensive stretches of blowdowns. Our forestry work back home often occurred in burn areas, where downed trees are the norm. We have hiked in places where we had to walk over one thousand trees in less than a mile, lifting our legs high and ducking low. Over and over and over again. However, the trees in Glacier Peak were of a far larger magnitude, making the small spruce back home look like toothpicks. We descended to lower elevations near the Suiattle River, where ample water and moderate temperatures had combined to allow for the growth of massive trees. The largest were Western red cedars, some of which we estimated at more than 20 feet in diameter (at breast height).

While it was awe-inspiring to see the trees upright, these same trees presented a significant challenge where they'd fallen across the trail. Over the course of three days, we navigated around them, going upslope, downslope, crawling below, clambering over, and occasionally going well around the downed obstacles. Fortunately, we didn't have to make any adjustments with Din, and she didn't seem to mind all the excess movement. She would put her hands up, resting on top of the pack, leaning forward with active eyes, curious to see what we were doing and what came next. Some stretches were so dense with blowdown that we couldn't make it a hundred yards without going over multiple trees, while others allowed us to go nearly a mile with nothing blocking our path. Alana took to counting how many blowdowns we passed, giving up at one point after counting nearly 200 in less than one day. Surprisingly, our daily mileage wasn't affected, but the climbing and scrambling over hundreds of trees left us sapped of our energy by the end of each day.

When we reached camp each evening, it was Din's turn to explore. She'd crawl around the dirt, examining rocks and sticks and fallen logs, while Alana and I attended to our nightly chores. Din would walk along the sides of logs, steadying herself against them, sometimes crawling over them, tossing aside broken pieces. Din was clearly pleased with her adventures, offering us a running commentary of her discoveries, babbling in a language only she could understand with a smile spread across her face. When it was bedtime, she would sometimes try to escape the tent, having figured out how to crawl in and out through the gaps between the mid's fabric and the ground. We encouraged her to move as much as possible, with the hope that all the activity would expend her energy, tiring her out and leading to a more restful night's sleep for all of us.

For most thru-hikers, a night's rest was their salvation, a solid eight to ten hours during which they could lie flat, zone out, recover, and recharge—no matter how difficult the day was, they could almost always be assured of a good night's sleep. For us new parents, on the other hand, night offered no respite. By the start of the trail, Din had not once slept through the night, still waking about two to three times most nights and occasionally more.

We had found at home that if Din didn't notice Alana's presence, she would go back to sleep far more easily and wouldn't wake as frequently. Since we co-slept, that usually meant that at the first signs of Din waking, Alana would leap from the bed to the floor, dragging an extra blanket down with her as I soothed Din back to sleep. On the trail, however, the thirty-some square feet of our tent made such a strategy impossible, meaning Din was waking even more, with the expectation of Alana feeding her back to sleep. If we weren't camped close to anyone, I'd put Din on my chest to calm her while Alana tried to hide beneath our shared quilt. But if others were nearby, we (mainly me) felt bad and, not wanting to disturb the others with our baby's wailing, would have Alana feed Din and serve as a human pacifier, often resulting in Din nursing through the night. Neither situation was ideal, both resulting in us waking up frequently and missing the restorative sleep we so direly needed.

After months of broken sleep, it wasn't unusual for Alana to mention that she could use a nap, which she did one day while we were heading up some switchbacks within a pine forest. I had looked at the map earlier and had my eyes on a good break spot about three miles farther along. Heading there would set us up well for the rest of the day. As we continued up the switchbacks, Din started pulling at Alana's hair, and I could tell that Alana was getting frustrated. This wasn't new—Din had started doing this months earlier, leading Alana to consider cutting off all of her hair before the trip. When combined with fatigue and physical exertion on the trail, Din's habit became especially frustrating. About half a mile later, we came across a side trail that led to some campsites up a hill. Alana wanted to rest there, but I argued for continuing to the spot I had picked earlier. Doing so would get most of our climbing out of the way and shorten the distance to that night's camp. Reluctantly, Alana agreed, and we stumbled on.

We entered an alpine bowl, the trees shrinking in size as we crossed small snowmelt streams. Summer had not yet arrived here, evident by the clusters of willows along the path that had yet to bud. Between the heat, the elevation gain, and our compounding fatigue, our energy levels were low. I had a lump in my throat as we continued, continually checking the GPS to see how far we were from the break spot. The "quick three miles" had dragged on, thanks to an uphill climb and more obstacles en route. Thinking we were going to be stopping soon, we had also forgone filling our empty water bottles, leaving us more dehydrated and crankier with each step.

About a third of a mile from our stopping point, we reached another fallen tree. Din started fussing—and Alana lost it.

"*ARRRGGGHHH!*" she yelled, taking her trekking pole and slamming it violently on the log. "You always do this!"

"Woah, woah, take a breath. It's okay," I said, holding my hands up and trying to calm her down.

Her eyes blazed with anger: "No! You never listen to me. This wouldn't happen if you just listened!"

Standing in the middle of the trail, I took my pack off, urging her to do the same. Din started to cry.

"It's okay. It's okay. Breathe with me. Let's take off the pack, and I'll take Din," I said

After a minute of protest, Alana took off her pack and I grabbed Din. It took a few moments for both of us to regain composure, but we continued onward, my pack on my back and Din in my arms. Upon reaching our goal, we turned off the trail to rest at some campsites. Alana descended to a spot lower on the hill to rest and have some time to herself, while Din and I played with pinecones, grasses, and low-growing plants higher on the slope.

It had made no difference for us if we took a break at one spot or another, but I had insisted on going forward to *my* spot. But at what cost? We had made it an additional two-plus miles, but we had stopped at a spot no better than the one Alana had suggested earlier, when she first needed a break. It seemed like the only things we had gained were an increased level of fatigue and marital strife. I felt uneasy and ashamed that there was nothing positive to show for the push, and that I'd let my ego do the talking once again. After an hour, Alana joined Din and I higher up the hill, saying that she wasn't proud of how she'd expressed her frustration. I apologized too, and at least for the moment, peace was restored. It was clear that the trail had only accentuated the points of contention in our relationship.

The next day, we met Jim from California,[1] who had been section-hiking for ten years and was now on his final section, moving northbound. He was out with his friend Rich from the United Kingdom. As we talked, Jim dangled one of his pack's shoulder straps out over his arm, resting the heavy load. While talking about his various trips on the trail, Jim said, "There are people out here going like twenty to twenty-five miles per day. I've heard of people trying to go thirty-plus miles per day in the desert. I'm like, 'Fuck you. Did you even see anything?'"

Common topics of contention among hikers are those of distance and style. Like Jim, there are some who take it as a personal affront that others travel farther, faster, and lighter than they do, as if they can't fathom how anyone could enjoy traveling more than fifteen miles per day. The complaint does have some basis, as there are "spreadsheet hikers" focused solely on maximizing their miles and who pay little mind to the areas they are traveling through, not able to name more than a couple plants or animals in the surrounding ecosystem. But going farther each day doesn't have to mean a death march or that you're ignoring what's around you, just like traveling at a slower pace doesn't magically bestow you with a wealth of ecological and geographical knowledge. In fact, with regards to "death marches," it's often just the opposite, as the farther you can travel each day, the less you have to carry in food and water, meaning you can in turn move more quickly, covering more ground....

The premise also ignores each person's preferences, like the idea that some *prefer* moving and walking over taking long breaks and/or spending lots of time at camp. As some might say (although the phrase is somewhat grating to me), "Hike your own hike."

---

1. Not his real name.

Two days into the Glacier Peak Wilderness, the trail wove through a stand of towering Western red cedars and over several more blowdowns before finally climbing back up into the alpine. There, we were welcomed by stunning views of the glaciated Mount Baker. The sound of cascading water filled the alpine basin around us as snowmelt from on high coursed through rocky channels to the valley below. We pushed through willow stands growing along the runoff streams, carefully hopping from rock to rock to reach the dry trail on the other side. While resting on a grassy slope, we watched fighter jets from a nearby naval base blow by overhead.

That night, we didn't have many options for camping, eventually finding a tucked-away spot near the rushing, glacier-fed Milk Creek, where others had mentioned the existence of a "one-man mouse army." While preparing dinner, I watched as mice ran over roots and around trees. Weary and not interested in dealing with them during the night, I pitched our mid as close to the ground as possible, in an effort to minimize any access points. We had run out of fuel the day before, so I cold-soaked some potatoes and dried morels that we had harvested near our home earlier in the summer.

Halfway through the meal, Alana wondered, "Don't you have to cook morels?"

"No, it's fine." I answered. "People eat them raw. I think you only have to cook them if you're eating them in large quantities."

By the end of the meal, Alana's stomach was bothering her. Fifteen minutes later my own stomach started to churn, leaving me nauseous. With Din asleep, we went to bed early, hoping to sleep it off. But the queasiness prevented any rest, resulting in us staring up at the green fabric of the tent, praying for relief. Mine came after about thirty minutes, when my stomach told me I needed to go outside ASAP. With the last bit of twilight on the horizon, I stumbled through the shadows to a fire pit, hunched over, and vomited up my dinner, mushrooms and all. As I lay down back in the tent, my stomach was content once more. The tent's zipper opening broke the surrounding silence shortly thereafter as Alana followed in my footsteps. Relieved, we fell fast asleep. We woke the next morning, having made it throughout the night without any visits from the local "army." I guess we'd paid our tribute.

Our sluggishness that morning, combined with a lengthy uphill to start the day, had us taking a long, early break to swim and relax in the alpine at Mica Lake, its grassy shores an oasis in comparison to the glaciers and boulder-strewn slopes above. Snow from the previous winter covered the rocks on the far side of the lake, melting into the crisp, clear water below. Alana and I took a dip while Din climbed up some small boulders. Refreshed and content, Alana lay out on a rock, basking in the sun. While Alana relaxed, Din was full of activity, crawling around the shore and standing for brief intervals, using the rocks to bring herself up before letting go for a few seconds each time.

Toward the end of the day, we came upon the glacial Kennedy River. Most rivers and creeks that we'd passed had bridges or were small trickles, but sans bridge and stretching twenty-five yards wide, this would be our first major crossing on the PCT. I first scouted downstream to see if there were a downed log or some boulders to cross on without having to enter the water, but no such luck. Some other hikers had just crossed from the other direction and pointed out what they thought was the best route directly through the water. With no sandbars or boulders to break up the crossing, I tried by myself first, the water reaching the lower portion of my thigh in the deepest section, and then dropped my pack on the far side and returned for Alana and Din. The water moved swiftly enough to require me to focus and place an emphasis on finding stable footing. While watching on shore, one woman had incredulously asked Alana, "You're doing that with a baby?" Having forded hundreds of rivers in Alaska, we were comfortable with our ability in the water and determining what was safe. While it wasn't a hop across, this river seemed more than manageable for us as a family.

The standard recommendation for safe river crossings is to unclip your pack's hip belt and chest strap so that you're not attached to it in the event of any issues. If you end up getting swept downstream, this allows you to lose the pack and avoid getting dragged under. With Din on my back, that wasn't an option. Instead, I tightened the straps of her carrier, Alana grabbed onto the back, and we forded across once more. The rushing water, while somewhat unnerving to us given the circumstances, seemed to have no effect on Din, who quietly observed what we were doing without a peep of excitement or displeasure. Safe on the other side with our shoes dripping wet, we squished and squashed a few more miles down the trail and established camp.

The latter half of the Glacier Peak Wilderness section proved to be just as eventful as the first. We swam in alpine lakes and trekked along ridges during the day, watching badgers run through alpine meadows and listening to marmots whistling among the rocks. Near the creeks and streams, small purple butterflies rested on the trail, flying off as a group once we neared. Each bend seemed to reveal a new, grand vista, showcasing the splendor of Mount Baker, Red's Pass, and our first glimpse of the giant Mount Rainier, the highest peak in the Pacific Northwest standing alone at 14,411 feet.

Emerging from the forest, above the shelter of the trees, I began experiencing some pain in my left hand one morning and noticed it becoming swollen. Alana thought it was some type of allergic reaction—maybe I had brushed against cow parsnip. I took some Zyrtec, but my hand kept swelling throughout the day, to the point that it grew to the size of a softball, rendering it more or less useless and preventing me from making a fist. Not long after, one of Alana's hands started hurting as well, and we realized it was the sun. With our skin exposed all day, we had gotten sun poisoning. We wet bandanas, wrapping them around our hands. Almost immediately, the swelling went down and function was restored.

Our spirits soared as we exited Glacier Peak Wilderness the following day—our eighth on the trail—thrilled to return to what we hoped was a better-maintained trail, free of thick brush and blowdowns. Taking advantage of the good conditions, we sailed on into the ski resort at Stevens Pass for a resupply, picking up our food boxes and marking the completion of another section. Only a week into our journey, we already had our hands full, still acclimating to life on the trail and struggling to get adequate rest. While Alana and I battled early symptoms of fatigue, it was clear that at least one of us was flourishing: Din.

8

Cheeks

Stevens Pass to Snoqualmie Pass, Washington
Snoqualmie Pass to Naches, Washington
July 16–July 25 172 miles

B efore the trip, we hadn't done much deep reading about
the trail and the areas it traveled through. As a result,
neither of us had much of an idea about what to expect in terms
of the scenery or the terrain, nor the difficulty of each section.
This lack of knowledge fostered a sense of wonder, as each mile
brought new surprises. One of the two books I had skimmed
was *The Pacific Crest Trail: A Hiker's Companion.*[1] While I
had read an overview of each section, the descriptions of these
unfamiliar places jumbled together in my memory. I vaguely
remembered the author discussing one section in Northern
Washington that she described as one of the trail's toughest, especially for southbounders, until reaching the Sierras. I couldn't
pinpoint exactly which one it was, but I'd convinced myself it
was from Stehekin to Stevens Pass. Well then, mission accomplished! With that section behind us, I figured there should be
nothing hindering our progress until California.

The truth was, the author had been describing the very section we were about to embark upon: Stevens Pass to Sno-

---

1. The other was *The Pacific Crest Trail: A Visual Compendi-
um.* Highly recommended!

qualmie Pass. Over the course of a few days, our legs were put to the test with a grueling pattern of ascending 3,000 feet up lengthy, steep passes, dropping back down to the valley floor, and then climbing back up again. This cycle continued relentlessly, seemingly never ending, and our pace was slower than anticipated; the climbs proved to be more challenging than the blowdowns in Glacier Peak, exacerbated by the extra weight of our newly restocked packs and fatigue from previous sections. Alana took the challenges in stride, visibly unaffected by our new obstacles. I, however, fared less well. After setting up camp one evening, I found myself shivering uncontrollably. Alana quickly helped dress me in all my clothes, wrapped me in our quilt, and built a fire. Moments like this made me deeply appreciate not only having a companion but one who could be relied upon in case of an emergency.

Further compounding these challenges was the lack of available water. We had become accustomed to crossing creeks and rivers every few miles, drinking our fill of the abundant water along the way. But all that changed in Southern Washington, with stretches of ten-plus miles without any sources of running water. Meanwhile, the failure of our water filter only intensified the situation. Prior to the trip, a friend had offered us his Steripen, a battery-powered UV water purifier. We were skeptical at first, wondering how long it would last, but upon hearing that they go for thousands of liters, it seemed like an easy choice. Only two weeks into our trip, however, we had already started to experience problems. The Steripen flashed an error code, but without access to internet, we could only guess what it meant. Finally, atop a high pass, we found a rare spot of cell service and were able to do some troubleshooting, only to find that the code indicated a dead battery. We had made the mistake of conflating the lifetime of the UV light with that of the batteries, which only lasted about ten days of daily use. Without any spare batteries or a backup filter, we were out of options.

Without a functioning filter, we became a lot more selective about our water sources, looking for flowing water, off the trail and as close to the source as possible. Unfortunately, these were hard to come by. Hesitant to drink from stagnant lakes and ponds, we carried what we could from more reliable sources. When that ran out, we went without. Mid-July brought some of Washington's warmest and driest weather, and without water, we baked under the harsh midsummer sun. Parched, we had no choice but to march on, our thoughts consumed by fantasies of water and our efforts focused on reaching the next stream as quickly as possible.

While we were thirsty and worried about how prolonged water scarcity might affect breastfeeding, Din appeared unaffected by our circumstances. At least for the time being, her milk supply was secure, leaving her to take in her surroundings. During the day, she sat in her perch high in her pack, head constantly on a swivel, looking at all the things passing by. This was often accompanied by her commentary, a seemingly endless stream of babbling and assorted noises strung together. Alana and I would often repeat them back to her and to each other, going miles down the trail while parroting our baby. However, Din still had her limits. Eventually, the novelty of the new sights would wear off or she would grow tired and start to fuss. Often, we could entertain her by giving her a large rock. She'd carry it in her hand, looking it over before finally sticking it in her mouth to use as a chew toy. When she got fed up with the rock, she'd either drop it out of the pack or stash it in her secret pocket, a small space between her harness straps and the pack frame.

Around this time, we discovered that Din had an affinity for jerky. This worked as our greatest pacifier, a panacea for when the rocks no longer proved a salve for her fussiness. We'd carry pieces in our hip-belt pockets, passing it back to her while cruising down the trail. She'd reach for the jerky, stick a piece in her mouth, take it out after a few moments, and then stick it back in, repeating this routine until the meat was soft enough for her to swallow. Between jerky and rocks, we had no shortage of teething materials. Add in all the dirt, sticks, pinecones, and boulders, and we had a full play set.

If all else failed, we'd take to singing, creating some of the most joyful moments of the trip for Alana and I. Walking down the trail, we would belt out, "The wheels on the bus go round and round, round and round, round and round...." and "Din went over the mountain, Din went over the mountain, Din went over the mountain, and what do you think she saw? She saw another mountain, she saw...."[2] Over and over and over again. We'd sing other songs from memory and make up songs of our own. Between trying to get Din to nap, calm her down when she was fussing, and singing her to sleep, we were singing those songs a couple dozen times a day. Uphill, downhill, day, night, water or no water—the conditions and time of day didn't matter.

There did seem to be a "pumpkin time," or "purgatory hour" as another thru-hiker called it, when Din became sick of being in the pack but was not yet ready to sleep. All our usual tricks would fail then, and our only recourse was to take her out of the pack. This meltdown seemed to always occur when we were on the final two miles to camp, during a steep uphill climb. So, inevitably, we'd find ourselves singing "The Wheels on the Bus" for the umpteenth time that day, trying to eke out the words in between breaths. Those days, we could never reach camp soon enough.

---

2. To the tune of "For He's a Jolly Good Fellow."

By this stage of our journey, about 10 days and around 200 miles into our trip, we had encountered several hundred thru-hikers traveling in both directions. To our surprise, the vast majority wore headphones, tuned out from the surrounding environment and absorbed in their Spotify playlist or podcasts they'd downloaded in the last town. The same was true whether the passing hikers were alone or within a group, and each traveled absorbed in their own world. We found it disheartening to see them muting at least one of their senses. Instead of being immersed in the stimuli of their surroundings, their attention was focused elsewhere, on some story from *This American Life,* one of their favorite songs on their playlist, or an audiobook dialogue. Listening so intently, I wondered if they ended up muting their other senses. *What did they miss seeing or smelling with those earbuds in?*

Don't get me wrong—I have nothing against podcasts, audiobooks, or music. I have done more than my fair share of listening over the years. But something like hiking the PCT—what should be a once-in-a-lifetime immersive experience—doesn't seem like the time or the place. By listening to what was around us, we became attuned to our surroundings. Hearing the wind's nuances gave an indication of the type of forest we were in—like an aspen forest where the wind fluttered through the leaves, or among the pines and cedars where the wind roared like waves. Birds sang to us throughout the day, the songs of the white crowned sparrow and the Swainson's thrush throughout Washington reminding us of home. Then there was the multitude of calls from ravens and eagles soaring high overhead; when we passed through logging or burn areas, their absence was just as notable. Miles without water led us to strain our ears for the sound of rushing streams. The sound of our footsteps changed as well, from the soft thud of our trail runners falling on the thick duff of pine forests to the clatter of our footfalls on rocky terrain.

Near the Waptus River in the Okanogan-Wenatchee National Forest, we had been playing leapfrog with another hiker
throughout the day. Close to camp, Alana stopped to feed Din
and I marched on, in search of water. Before I left, the other
hiker, with headphones in and music blaring, had just passed
us. I followed in his steps no more than a couple minutes later.
A half mile farther, I heard the scratching of bark in the trees.
Instantly recognizing the sound, I turned to see a bear cub
climbing a tree just thirty yards off the trail, with mom at the
base. I readied myself and let loose a loud, "Hey!" The bears
quickly scampered off into the alders. I waited there until Alana
and Din arrived. We saw the other hiker not long after, and I
asked him if he had seen the bears.

"Bears?" he responded.
"Yeah, they were back maybe a mile or so, just off to the left
side of the trail. A sow and cub."
"Didn't," was his sole response.

The headphones were symbolic of a larger trend in the outdoors, the pervasive use of electronic devices in the backcountry, something that's become ever more prevalent as smartphone use has become endemic within the modern world. Once
thought of as a haven or retreat from these devices, smartphone
use in the backcountry is now almost as pervasive as in the
city—at least this was the case to our eye. On the PCT, nearly
everyone relied on GPS mapping software through one app or
another, in lieu of paper maps. The devices also served as cam-
eras, journals, web browsers, entertainment centers, and more.
Cell-phone coverage had expanded over the years to the extent
that *not* being in range for at least some point during the day
was unusual. The available coverage was hard to ignore, leading
some to place calls to loved ones while walking, and texting
others on breaks and in camp. As little as fifteen years ago, prior

to the widespread use of smartphones, such practices were far more difficult or impossible, but nonetheless, people managed to thru-hike the PCT all the same, the lack of connection to civilized society proving no overwhelming burden to their quest.

We were caught up in the trend ourselves. With a baby in tow and limited time and energy, we'd decided to expedite our planning process by using FarOut as our mapping app for navigation purposes. On the trail, we'd frequently check our position on the app, pulling out our phones to see how many miles before our next break, water source, or camp. Others would use it to an even greater, almost nonsensical degree, relying on it to pinpoint their location within feet, to seek out specific campsites or water sources, things they could have easily seen with their eyes. We'd all put our faith in software, keeping us tethered to the digital world, trading immersion in nature for ease and convenience. By keeping one foot elsewhere, we had shunned the vulnerability that comes with opening ourselves up to the solitary wilderness experience and the adversity and uncertainty that accompany it. *What had we lost in the process?*

Despite the lack of headphones, I'm no Buddha, and my thoughts didn't always stay in the present. Unfocused, they would stray far and wide, reliving events from grade school or high school. I also had "what if" thoughts about the future concerning my loved ones like Alana and Din, thoughts that sometimes brought me to tears. I thought about what we'd do after the trail: initial thoughts about writing this book, about building an addition on our home in Arctic Alaska, about getting to hunt and garden again, about exploring our home state. Then, like everyone else, we both had plenty of thoughts on the miles and logistics of the trail: *Should we refill our water at the next creek or wait? Should we take a break soon or try for a few more miles?* And increasingly, I fantasized about the specialty foods that awaited us in the next town: burritos, milkshakes, burgers, cinnamon rolls, and other calorie laden delicacies.

Alana's mind raced along as well, but to the tune of numbers. As we walked, she counted the logs we crossed, the steps she took, how many diapers we had on hand, and how long we had until Din needed to sleep again. She was always the more musically oriented one in our relationship, and her thoughts reflected that, with old songs filling her mind until she couldn't take them anymore, trying to think of anything but their lyrics. And finally, there were thoughts related to her personal needs, like whether she was getting enough food and water, to support not only herself but Enedina as well.

These subtle differences between our thoughts spoke to the difference in our experience and how, from early on, our views of the trip were slowly diverging. We were both worn down, and I had clearly underestimated the difficulty of doing the trail while sleep deprived and carrying heavier packs. But each of us perceived these challenges in different ways. To me, they seemed like obstacles merely to push and occasionally suffer through as part of the journey; this framing allowed me to hold a positive view of our trip, despite any struggles. But to Alana, who was not just taking care of herself but Din as well, these struggles were an existential threat to her and our child's well-being. As such, to her, the extra challenges were not welcomed, and rightfully so, making for an experience that was often less than fun. Uncertain how to deal with the situation, she bottled up her worries, hoping for a change in circumstances. But with only each other to depend on, there didn't seem to be reprieve coming any time soon.

After a couple of weeks, it was readily apparent that kids, let alone babies, were a rarity on the trail. This led to some amusing encounters, especially when Din was wailing away. A baby crying is not something that most people are accustomed to hearing in the forest and mountains, and passersby often mistook her cries for those of a mountain lion, prey in distress, or a bleating mountain goat. Most people we met would ask us if we were out for the weekend or just a section, or comment how nice it was that we were getting the "little guy" out for the day. Upon hearing that we were thru-hiking, they usually peppered us with questions about logistics and concerns about whether Din was enjoying it. We'd receive heaps of thanks and praise for setting such an example. Others asked to take our picture. We knew our trip was unconventional, but neither of us had imagined that others would draw so much inspiration from it.

Meanwhile, Alana had already made a handful of friends on the trail, people we passed or met while stopping for breaks. Alana would exchange stories with them and ask about their trail experiences. She has the gift of being able to empathize and connect with people, quickly endearing herself to others and forming meaningful relationships. There was a marked difference between when we were traveling on our own versus when we were near her new trail friends. In their company, she became visibly excited and exuded energy, thrilled to be around those who were doing something similar. When it was just us, I could tell she sometimes felt relegated to her role as a mother, burdened with a seemingly endless list of responsibilities. It was hard not to get caught up in all the chores, and our share of the burden was far from equal, with Alana often shouldering the majority. However, spending time with friends, both new and old, provided her with a significant mental break.

Din was the ultimate ice-breaker—the sight of her along the trail would elicit a reaction from most hikers, sometimes sparking a longer conversation, other times brief encouragement or a simple smile. Fittingly, she was the first of us to get a trail name. On long thru-hikes, it's common for hikers to adopt or be assigned nicknames, which usually come from a story, characteristic, or action unique to that person. So far, we had met Marmot Punch, Milkman, Happy Mule, Tit Punch, Ted Talks, Starburst, and Dog Treat. In Snoqualmie Pass, we spent a night at the Washington Alpine Club's Guye Cabin, waiting for a package to arrive and catching up on town chores. We exchanged stories with other hikers, and Din, now 10 months old, learned to wave for the first time. Over a communal dinner of spaghetti, Din practiced her newfound skill, waving to every-one in the room. She was the center of attention and ate it up. By the end of the night, she had acquired her own trail name: "Cheeks."

We were back on the trail the next day with more of a whim-per than a bang. Heavy packs, loaded with five days of food, slowed us down as we made our way up the ski slopes of the Summit at Snoqualmie and back into the forest. Nearing the slope's summit, Alana grew disheartened and frustrated. Her Achilles tendon was bothering her, making each step a painful ordeal. She wasn't sure that carrying on was prudent, and con-templated waiting a few days for it to improve. I suggested swapping packs. She was reluctant at first, but then set Din down while I went through both packs, redistributing food and gear to make hers a lot lighter. Loaded down and lightened up, we continued on.

The previous three sections had gotten us accustomed to big mountains, lakes, and large views. That changed as we made our way south into our next section. Expansive "wilderness" areas were replaced with private and national-forest logging tracts. The trail wound through stretches of monoculture for-est, where uniform rows of a single pine species lined each hill-side. The area seemed to be ecologically and spiritually dead.

Just like a full-growth mature forest isn't ideal for any living species, neither is a single-species forest. Silence filled the area, broken only by the breeze. The sounds of birdsong and running water that we had come to cherish were noticeably absent.

The lighter pack along with some stretching had helped Alana's Achilles, but we had traded it for pain of my own. Tightness in my IT band resulted in pain with each step, especially on the downhills. We descended three miles from a windy Sourdough Gap, crossing Highway 410 into Mount Rainier National Park, where we were greeted by rain. We stopped under some large, overhanging pine boughs to put on our rain jackets. As we went farther into the park, the wind increased, forcing us to stay on the move to keep warm. Clouds enshrouded the mountains, so there wasn't much for us to see beyond the dripping trees and our immediate surroundings.

We had bundled Din up in all the clothes she had: pants, a jacket, winter hat, handmade wool booties from family friends in Alaska, some mittens, and a rain jumpsuit. She didn't like the mittens and kept throwing them off, so we had to stop every few minutes to rewarm her cold hands. Despite the cold, she was undisturbed, babbling away and showing no signs of displeasure. Toward the end of the day, Alana was feeling tired and beaten down, so she trekked the last few miles downhill slowly, while I went ahead with Din to establish camp. The rain had stopped, there was no wind, and we were protected in the trees. Content, we all turned in to bed early, hoping for some rest.

A few nights earlier at the Guye Cabin, Din had nearly slept through the night for the first time in her life. Alana and I wondered if the mattress was responsible for the improvement. Willing to try almost anything in hopes of more sleep, we changed our sleeping arrangement within the tent. Previously, Din shared with us our thin, closed-cell-foam pads, which offered a mere quarter inch of foam cushioning. Each night from then on, we would repurpose our extra clothing, such as rain jackets and pullovers, fashioning a makeshift mattress for her. This new setup provided significantly more cushioning, and we hoped it would facilitate better sleep going forward.

But that night would not be one of them. After waking to Din crying earlier in the night, I was nudged awake again by Alana. The rain had resumed, and we heard drops beating down on the nylon fabric above us.

"There's water in the tent," Alana said. I sat up half-asleep and fumbled around in the dark, trying to figure out what she was talking about. I felt around our sleeping pads, but didn't find any source of wetness, so I mumbled, "It's just from the tent itself."

"No! I can feel it on my leg. It's under me." With Din asleep on her chest, she was unable to investigate.

Another round of fumbling, this time on the outside of Alana's sleeping pad, and sure enough, there was a steady stream of water running through the tent. Lacking a tent floor and with only our thin foam pads separating us from the ground, we should have expected this. Yet, accustomed to the typically dry conditions, we'd grown complacent, giving no thought to potential rain and running water when choosing campsites.

After I confirmed our predicament with my headlamp, Alana exclaimed, "You never listen! You ignored me the first time and now everything is soaked."

Still half-asleep, I was very confused, and asked, "What first time?"

"I woke you up earlier and told you there was water in the tent, and you just mumbled something and kept sleeping."

"I was asleep, I don't remember that at all. I wasn't actually awake."

"Ugh, whatever."

Alana grabbed Din and went outside, standing in the rain as I tried to find a dry spot to place our sleeping pads.

"Are you done yet?"

"I'm working as fast as I can."

By angling the sleeping pads into the corner, I was able to find the sole dry spot away from any running water. We got back into our quilt, the foot box soaked, and tried to go back to sleep. I slept little from then on, listening to the rain fall onto the tent. The water had soaked some of our clothes, and the moist air prevented the diapers we had washed the day before from drying out.

Everyone besides Din was grumpy come morning, and Alana and I traveled the first two miles of trail without saying a word to each other. We had only spent two weeks on trail, but we were already physically and emotionally spent, thanks to the elements, exhaustion, water issues, and other stressors. Adding to all that, a night that ended in our gear soaked, sleep disrupted, and our relationship further strained felt like a kick in the gut.

Away from the lofty peaks and amidst the high trees of the forest flats at the Bumping River, Din had started crying, so we stopped and sat on a log.

I asked Alana, "Can we talk about this please?"

"We should just quit when we get to Naches this afternoon."

"What?! Why?"

"Because this is pointless—the same stuff just keeps happening."

Alana's desire to end the trip was unexpected and caught me off guard. Sure, I thought, we had experienced plenty of challenges so far, but we were still relatively fresh to the trail and still learning from our mistakes. None of this seemed like anything that couldn't be overcome—at least, that's how I saw it.

We spent the next fifteen minutes talking past each other, our conversation halted only by the arrival of a couple across the river. Still wrung out from our talk, we tried to engage politely in their conversation, exchanging pleasantries and small talk about the trail. After a few minutes, we decided to scamper up the log spanning the water and cross the river. There wasn't much progress in our discussion but somehow, we had come to an understanding. With Din on my back, we hiked an uneventful fourteen more miles along flat terrain past meadows, lakes, and ponds to the road near Naches. Here, at the very least, we could put our water issues to rest, buying a new water filter at the gas station in town, giving us one less thing to worry about.

Over the following days, we noticed a change in attitude among the people we passed, soon realizing that we were encountering the first wave of northbound thru-hikers. Common trail etiquette across the country is to greet, or at the very least acknowledge, others as you pass. There are also right-of-way guidelines, most explicitly on hills, where the person hiking uphill has the right of way. The first group of northbounders was notable because none of them followed any of these practices. Many refused to move when it was our right of way, forcing us to step off the trail, while others ignored our greetings. It was more strange than anything else.

To one oncoming hiker, I said "Morning!" as I stepped off the trail. He just looked at me blankly and asked, "What?"

"Morning," I repeated.

He continued to look at me blankly, and then looked down, saying a quick, "Thank you very much," after he'd passed. This was relatively polite compared to others who met our greetings with silence or brushed past, not yielding an inch of trail. Alana grew frustrated, venting "They're not gonna give us the right of

way even with a baby?! I'm not going to stop for the next ones."
And she didn't. For the next few days on uphill stretches, Alana
continued without yielding the trail when we had the right of
way. This led to some tense moments, with some northbound
hikers walking within feet of her before realizing she wasn't
going to step aside.

Almost none of those we passed looked like they were enjoying the trail; they seemed to be trudging on out of obligation,
having already walked the majority of the trail and wanting just
to see it through. Their long faces, vacant stares, and lethar-
gic shuffling communicated their diminished spirits eloquent-
ly, without a word being spoken. Some 1,500 miles into their
2,650-mile trip, they were weary from the long days, the weeks
of contending with snow in the Sierras, the logistics of skipping
around snow-submerged trails, and the hordes of mosquitoes
in Oregon. To us, they appeared like zombies. Neither of us had
any interest in reaching such a state, and we agreed to end our
trip if either of us ended up feeling so strung out.

9

Wilderness?

Naches to Trout Lake, Washington
July 26–July 29 66 miles

C oming from Alaska, we had ample experience in deep
wilderness environments, having traveled, worked, and
recreated in places where the nearest road or town was hundreds
of miles away and there were zero signs of human presence.
These are places where any help was days away and that leave you
questioning where you sit on the food chain. We had no reason
to believe that the PCT could match what Alaska had to offer.
The population density of Washington, Oregon, and California
is significantly higher than Alaska's; infrastructure is far more
abundant in the Lower 48, in terms of roads and services but
also things like trails. By my estimate, the 505 miles of trail that
the PCT covers through Washington alone equals more trail
mileage than can be found within all of Alaska. In other words,
Alaska has fewer trail miles than just one trail in Washington,
despite being more than twice the area of Washington, Oregon,
and California combined.

Even so, the PCT certainly crosses rugged terrain. As we
hiked, I gazed in awe at the steep slopes, thick brush, and piles of
downed trees just off the trail. Accustomed to traveling off-trail
and bushwhacking, I couldn't help but consider how difficult
it would be to walk in this area without a path. We had crossed
glacial rivers and creeks, ascended and descended steep passes,

and journeyed through dense forests, all made possible by this three-foot-wide strip of dirt cutting through the mountains. However, despite the ruggedness, we were dismayed to find that the areas we passed through were often far from wilderness or even immersive. Even the many congressionally designated Wilderness areas often left us feeling like we were walking through a suburban forest preserve, encountering signs of impact like crowds, devegetated campsites, and piles of toilet paper that we were far from accustomed to.

The Pacific Crest Trail came to fruition, after many years of advocacy, as part of the Wilderness Act of 1964, which along with creating dozens of official wilderness areas, established the National Trails System. The PCT was meant to be a continuous path across the country from north to south, from one border to the other, in wilderness or wilderness like environments. To achieve this, the trail travels where possible on public lands (national forests, national parks, etc.) and occasionally on easements through Native American reservations and private lands.

Connecting different segments together as linearly as possible, the travel corridor goes through a lot of less-than-breathtaking areas. Throughout Southern Washington, much of Oregon, and Northern California, the trail frequently passes through logging areas, some of which are actively being logged, leading to the presence of large machinery and damaged trails. Others had been logged recently or many years ago. Since the PCT is under a protective easement on these lands, it remains unlogged, while the surrounding areas may be clear-cut. Logging and national forests also mean roads, primarily for machinery and log transport, which we started crossing frequently in Southern Washington.

The high density of roads near the PCT and its proximity to major urban areas like Seattle meant we also encountered many people. On the busiest days, we'd see more than 100 over the course of the day. In our usual ten hours on trail, this amounted to us seeing someone roughly every five to six minutes. Throughout Washington, the average was around 60 people per day. It didn't matter if we were near the trailhead or 30 miles in—the crowds were everywhere. In comparison, hiking in forest preserves near my mom's home in suburban Chicago, we'd be unlikely to hit that number within a week, while in Alaska, we'd be unlikely to see 60 hikers in an entire summer.

The crowds weren't always comprised solely of other back-packers. One day, we shared the trail with an ultramarathon, which overlapped the PCT for 30 miles as part of its 100-mile course. The race was out and back, so we saw the same 130-plus runners twice. The passing of each runner required us to step off the trail every couple of minutes, significantly slowing our travel. Every six miles, we passed an aid station, whose volunteers kindly offered us snacks they had prepared for the runners.

We hit the peak of the northbound bubble[1] of hikers in the Goat Rocks Wilderness, just south of Naches. Many of the hikers we passed hyped up the popular, narrow segment of ridge known as the "Knife's Edge" and its sweeping views up high. "It's the greatest view I've ever seen in my life," one said. "My mind is still unable to comprehend what I saw," another remarked. Some warned us about the dangers of the narrow trail above, expressing concern about us going forward with a baby. A week earlier, at the Guye Cabin in Snoqualmie Pass, another hiker had told us about how he'd had to coach someone across the tight passage, the person so scared of traveling above the ridge's steep dropoffs that they'd frozen up. Wondering what lay in store, we trotted up the ridge into the fog, which lifted as we approached the precarious edge, revealing views of Mount

---

1. A mass of thru-hikers who have clustered together after weeks or months of hiking.

Rainier to the north, Mount Saint Helens to the west, and Mount Adams to the south. We kept waiting for the dangerous, narrow section to show itself, only to find that we had already passed it. The views were expansive, but throughout the day we passed more and more people, to the point where it started to take away from the experience. We would see people around each bend, leaving us few moments with a view or an area to ourselves.

All this traffic led to a greater impact on the trail and its surrounding areas. Campsites around lakeshores were abundant, with evidence of people camping right up to the lake's edge, contrary to best practices. Other sites and disturbed areas were regularly present, too. However, an even worse eyesore were the all-too-frequent instances where someone had relieved themselves and hadn't buried their waste and toilet paper. There seemed to be people on the trail who either didn't care about those who came after them or were shortsighted enough to think that their actions didn't have any effect. It wasn't just an aesthetic issue either. We found some of these piles within 100 feet of rivers, lakes, and other water sources, potentially introducing contamination.

I'm not of the mind that there ever really was a true wilderness, some utopian Eden in which humans were completely absent. Unlike the National Park Service, which adheres to a rigid, arbitrary standard of preservation wherein intensive human interaction is a relic of the past,[2] I believe humans *should* inhabit

---

2. Going as far as to remove, burn, and destroy pre-existing dwellings and evict people from their historical and ancestral homes. For those interested in reading more on the topic, I'd recommend the books *Wilderness and the American Mind* by Roderick Frazier Nash and *A Land Gone Lonesome* by Dan O' Neill.

natural, "wild" environments. These modern-day "wilderness" areas are the historical anomaly, capturing something that likely never has existed—a land without humans. How we go about conserving these areas in our modern age with large populations, tremendous societal wealth, and a strong desire among many to spend time in nature requires much contemplation. While increased development is eliminating nature closer to home, more people are being encouraged to take to the outdoors, forcing everyone to head to the same areas. In striving for widespread access to nature, aren't we despoiling the very thing we seek? Or is it that we are misguided, prizing romantic and awe-inspiring "wild" landscapes over those closer to home, which are in equal need of our consideration and care?

The PCT hadn't always been this busy. Since 2013, the number of permits issued for thru-hikes has increased 500 percent, going from around 1,000 per year to 5,000. That number isn't fully representative of traffic on the trail, as many don't end up using their permit for whatever reason or quit early on, plus there are day hikers and other users along its length that affect the numbers. In 2013, just under 250 people reported finishing the whole trail, while in 2022, there were about 1,000. A lot of the popularity stems from the book *Wild* by Cheryl Strayed, published in 2012, and the ensuing movie of the same name starring Reese Witherspoon. Both the book and movie were wildly successful, launching the trail into mainstream consciousness and, for many, creating a desire to follow in Cheryl's footsteps.

Don't get me wrong—we were obviously part of the crowd. It's like the person sitting in their car complaining about traffic, while failing to recognize that they, too, are part of the traffic. These areas are public lands, owned collectively by all citizens and open to our use. To manage the growing number of long-distance hikers, the nonprofit Pacific Crest Trail Association created a permit system in 2013 to try to stem the flow. However, since this system only governs the start dates of hikers and lacks enforcement afterward, it falls well short of its goal, with crowds forming early on and big groups—the bubbles—traveling, resting, and camping together. Consequently, these beloved areas are suffering from overuse.

These differing landscapes and how they are treated and used speak to our conflicting perspectives on the land and our relationship to it as humans. For a mile, Alana, Din, and I would traverse designated wilderness, with little to no maintenance and defined as "where the earth and its community of life are untrammeled by man, where man himself is a visitor who does not remain."[3] But then, shortly thereafter, our path would lead us through a clear-cut, a stark contrast in which the land has been stripped yet still embodies the principle that humans are transient visitors, though in an extractive context in this case. Both landscapes reflect our modern view of nature and wilderness as entities separate from everyday human existence, places we visit but do not inhabit.

The term "wilderness" is a loaded one with various meanings, influenced by the era and perspective of each person. In early American history, wilderness represented unchartered territories ripe for conquest and exploitation, hostile lands needing to be tamed. Although the frontier era has long passed, this mentality lingers. Conversely, a romanticized view of wilderness emerged with the closing of the frontier and the increase of urbanization, valuing natural areas for their inherent beauty and integrity, not for their utility.

Both perceptions, however, are problematic in that they situate humans as entities residing apart from nature. Historically, humans were deeply integrated with their environments, coexisting with nature as seamlessly as any other species. Such was

---

3. From the Wilderness Act of 1964.

the case across the world, including in North America, where Native Americans resided as stewards of the land for thousands of years. Generally, with significantly lower human populations and densities than today, the land and its resources were used sustainably. This helped maintain a level of biodiversity and natural resources that sustained human populations for well over ten thousand years.

Ignoring this history, the official definition of wilderness, per the Wilderness Act of 1964, attempts to freeze in time an ecosystem that was only briefly without human presence. In the book *Uncommon Ground,* William Cronon argues:

> "The removal of Indians to create an 'uninhab-
> ited wilderness"—uninhabited as never before in
> the human history of the place--—reminds us just
> how invented, just how constructed, the Ameri-
> can wilderness really is....there is nothing natural
> about the concept of wilderness. It is entirely a
> creation of the culture that holds it dear, a prod-
> uct of the very history it seeks to deny. Indeed,
> one of the most striking proofs of the cultural
> invention of wilderness is its thoroughgoing era-
> sure of history from which it sprang."[4]

In modern society—disconnected from our roots and living in urban areas—we no longer see natural areas as a place where the materials used to sustain our lives come from. For most peo-ple, nature is somewhere we *go*, not somewhere we *live*. Cronon later writes how our constricted ideas of wilderness have led to

4. Cronon, William. *Uncommon Ground,* pp. 79–80.

this viewpoint, arguing, "Without our quite realizing it, wilderness tends to privilege some parts of nature at the expense of others. Most of us, I suspect, still follow the conventions of the romantic sublime in finding the mountaintop more glorious than the plains, the ancient forest nobler than the grasslands, the mighty canyon more inspiring than the humble marsh."

The trail culture among many thru-hikers (us included) often emphasized similar values, with a strong preference for grand mountain vistas and sublime landscapes, but markedly less enthusiasm for more ordinary areas like flat, scrubby forests. It seems we believed that our experiences were enriched by emphasizing the more picturesque aspects of our journeys, whether for spiritual fulfillment or baser notions like social-media appeal. Living on the trail marked a significant step toward immersing ourselves in the environment, as for months at a time, hundreds of us called the PCT our home. Yet, this coexistence wasn't flawless, with our gear, food, and supplies sourced from the industrialized world. As such, this integration was incomplete, leaving us more akin to transient visitors—like, say, clear-cut loggers—than true residents. In a way, this aspect spoke to the extremes of how we view ourselves within nature, as the thru-hiker lifestyle wasn't truly sustainable. We would all have to return to our lives elsewhere, where we would be unlikely to find the connections with the natural world we'd formed on the PCT.

With our mixed-up and often contradictory relationship to nature, and with user numbers in the outdoors booming, the challenge of balancing access and conservation remains. I'm not sure what the answer is, but I'd argue we need to return to balance, to a world in which those who see nature as something to exploit and conquer can give more thought to the long-term health and conservation of the entire ecosystem, while those who see nature as something to preserve and set aside can also see it as an environment that humans are a part of, can use, and can reside within. Meanwhile, a strict user-number quota in the busiest areas outdoors seems to be the only thing that could stem the tide, though I'm not sure it would be welcome.

Throughout our days, we would see birds, chipmunks, squirrels, and other small mammals like marmots. But despite covering hundreds of miles at all hours of the day, we rarely saw deer or other large mammals, let alone their tracks. The trail often meandered through higher elevations and alpine environments, which typically have lower animal densities, but the near absence of large wildlife was notable. It seemed that the heavy traffic had displaced the animals elsewhere.

Our experiences led my thoughts back home to Alaska, where most hunters take to their cars, ATVs, and boats, cruising the roads and rivers, hoping to spot something along the way. The animals become wise to this quickly and move outside the road and river corridors. For the individual willing to work harder and venture a little farther, abundant wildlife awaits. I was left with a similar feeling on the PCT. Perhaps just a mile off the trail, in either direction, we might find the wildlife we missed. Was the trail essentially just a hiker's autobahn?

All of this pointed to a lack of an ecological balance. We had gone to the woods to find that balance, but instead found it lacking, which reminded me of Lois Crisler's famous quip from her book *Arctic Wild* that "Wilderness without wildlife is just scenery." In Washington, the scales had been heavily weighted in the direction of humans, and other animals had been displaced as a result. We found what was left to be a place without a soul.

The national scenic trails, including the PCT, were established to offer "maximum outdoor recreation potential and for the conservation and enjoyment of the nationally significant scenic, historic, natural, or cultural qualities of the areas through which such trails may pass."[5] From our perspective, access has been prioritized at the expense of conservation. Is it worth waiting until the experience is degraded enough to tip the scales in the other direction? With the current ethos, what kind of experience are we leaving for future generations? *Encyclopedia Brittanica* defines conservation as the "study of the loss of Earth's biological diversity and the ways this loss can be prevented."[6] With this definition in mind, I was left wondering, what exactly is being conserved?

I wondered if anyone else had noticed what was missing. It was hard for me to imagine so, with so many hikers coming from urban areas. Was it that many simply lacked the exposure to intact ecosystems with which we're so blessed in Alaska? If you're used to the streets of Brooklyn, Seattle, or other metropolitan areas, it's easy to see how your perspective would be different. Replacing an overabundance of concrete with an overabundance of greenery, one might perceive the latter as wild. Yet within that greenery, there was an emptiness. This reminds me of the Grand Canyon and the Colorado River after the Glen Canyon Dam was put into place. To people familiar with what lay beneath the water within Glen Canyon, it was a tragedy.

---

5. Per The National Trails System Act of 1968. Amended in 2019.

6. Pimm, S. L. "conservation." *Encyclopedia Britannica*, January 8, 2024. https://www.britannica.com/science/conservation-ecology.

But for those who only saw and knew the reservoirs, there was nothing to mourn.

I was lucky enough to get exposure to intact ecosystems relatively early on, when I was 20 years old. My introduction to Alaska and the outdoors began in the summer of 2013, when I took that semester course with NOLS. We spent twenty-five days sea-kayaking in Prince William Sound, followed by fifty continuous days of backpacking and glacial mountaineering in Wrangell-Saint Elias National Park. Coming from Chicago, I was blown away by the vast scale of the land and the intact wilderness environment. During those fifty days, we encountered no roads or towns, only seeing a state trooper and our resupply pilot over the seven weeks. Returning home, I experienced an intense culture shock that lasted months and sent my mood spiraling downward. It was the most immersive experience of my life—unlike anything I had ever experienced—and permanently changed its course.

Prior to setting out on the PCT, I had hopes of finding something similar on the trail. But with all the above factors in play, it didn't seem likely. Even if there were fewer people and more animals as we hiked south, we were still passing through towns every three to five days. Expecting a level of immersion comparable to my Alaskan adventure was simply unreasonable. The landscapes were just too different.

10

Mount Adams

Mount Adams Wilderness, Washington
July 28–July 29

Throughout Washington, we often found ourselves racing to reach town on resupply days to get our food boxes before the post office closed, so that we wouldn't have to spend a night off-trail, waiting for them to reopen the next day. This meant our days often felt rushed, like we were being whisked away to fulfill our timetables. As a result, we ended up turning into our own version of spreadsheet hikers, focused on miles and timing to the detriment of our experience. Part of that was baked into our trip, as with the goal of completing the trail with Din, we couldn't afford to do side trips or spend exorbitant amounts of time on anything but forward progress. We weren't operating by just our own schedule, but also in line with Din's naps, her feedings, her diaper changes, and the daily ticking time bomb of how long she would be content in the pack. While other hikers could stop as they pleased, our circumstances made us feel like we didn't have much time each day to do anything but make forward progress if we were going to get through the mountains before the snowstorms arrived.

We met a couple of Europeans who were taking their time, spending six weeks going through Washington and exploring every side trail and whim that came their way. They were taking twice as long as us but were having the time of their lives.

Before we'd started, we'd had no puritanical notions of hiking every single mile of the trail, realizing that the journey was what was important. This was evident in us skipping the northern terminus and the sixty-mile out-and-back to get there. Instead, we tried to focus on where we were, not thinking of some far-off locale. But it was clear from our rushing that we still had lots to learn.

Although rare, there were some days when everything lined up and we found ourselves with extra time. In those cases, we embraced spontaneity, often whiling away an afternoon at some alpine lake. We'd drop our packs on shore, let Din out of her pack to crawl around and explore, and take turns swimming in the crystal-clear depths. After days of sweat, dirt, and grime, the water was refreshing, allowing us the opportunity to reenergize and reset. For a moment, we escaped the relentless march onward.

Such experiences brought about an epiphany. Alana and I had each come into the hike thinking that it was *our* trip, and that Din was along for the ride. However, the reality turned out to be the exact opposite. We were hiking *Din's* hike. She took priority, and everything we did served to best support her and allow her to thrive. Once we were underway and the on-trail logistics of thru-hiking with Din became clear, it seemed silly to think otherwise.

Years ago, when Alana was on the trail crew doing maintenance and improvements, she had envisioned a different journey. Back then, she never pictured doing the trail with a partner, let alone a baby. Her visions of the experience spoke more to the thrill of independence and being out on her own, testing herself in the wild. Consumed with preparations and care for Din prior to the trip, she (like myself) had not given a thought to how the trail experience might be different with an infant. It wasn't worse, but it was different—and certainly more complicated. And that took time to get accustomed to.

We thought about the trail on a larger scale frequently as we traveled the last couple hundred miles in Washington. Considering the surprisingly large crowds and the different style of experience, Alana wondered if it was worth carrying on or if we were better off just heading south to do something else, like biking through the unpopulated deserts of Mexico's Baja Peninsula on faint dirt tracks. Was it worth just calling it quits and finding something that was more novel and in line with what we wanted to do? I did some figuring and estimated that if we were at the peak of the northbound bubble, we'd have about two more weeks of a busy trail before it died back down to more reasonable levels somewhere in Central Oregon. For the moment, this seemed like a reasonable amount of time, and we opted to continue.

Despite the lack of a general sense of wilderness, there were still moments that were wild and made us feel alive. We were on the trail one evening around 6 p.m., looking to make miles to set ourselves up for resupply in the next town, when we came to the banks of Adams Creek. Silty glacial runoff from Mount Adams rumbled and tore through the gravel channels below the banks in front of us. The creek, 100 feet wide, was unlike any we'd seen on the trail, without any obvious way across. Most creeks without bridges had had large logs that had conveniently fallen across, or they'd been shallow enough to splash across without worry. But Adams Creek was a rushing torrent.

After finding no better option downstream (and with Din on my back), I hopped up onto a large log, walking along the trunk to a small gravel bar in the middle of the river. Two thin, scraggly pines lay across the next channel, spanning fifteen feet over the rushing water to dry ground on the far bank. Alana stood back on shore while I eyed the logs, testing their stability. I was filled with doubt. Balance going across would be paramount, and if Din got nervous and started wiggling in the pack, it could send us both into the churning water below. Alana offered to go first, and slowly began crossing to the other side. Then, Din began crying. I stepped up onto the logs, trying to soothe her while placing all my focus on maintaining my balance. My toes splayed out over the water, my shoes dampened by the froth just inches below. Alana said something on shore, but I didn't hear it, having blocked out all my senses to focus on the task at hand. The sound of rushing water filled my ears as I focused on the two feet in front of me. After a couple minutes of cautiously moving across, I took a big step onto a boulder, reaching dry ground once more. We took Din out of the pack, letting out a huge sigh of relief, and then we all embraced on shore.

In Mount Adams Wilderness, before reaching the town of Trout Lake, we met our first true NOBO. Until then, we had encountered only SNOBOs, as they liked to call themselves—NOBOs who'd skipped sections of the trail with high snow levels, leaving the SoCal desert and bypassing the immense snowpack in the Sierra to continue their hike from Chester, California, leaving the Sierras for later in the summer once the snow had melted. We were taking a break, sitting against a log snacking, when "The Alpinist" walked up and exclaimed, "You're doing this with a baby? That's incredible." We found out that he had hiked solo through the Sierras, often through deep snow where he'd postholed through to his waist, and we were quick to praise him. He demurred, saying, "I'm not sure about any of that that. Stubborn maybe, but what *you're* doing is impressive," adding, "I struggled coming up that last hill by myself; I couldn't imagine doing it with a baby."

By this stage of the trail, we were accustomed to receiving such compliments a few times a day. It was very flattering, and we always expressed gratitude for the kind words. In most circumstances, it'd be easy to see how something like this would go to our heads, leading to a sense of superiority or an air of pompousness. But any time we drifted toward self-admiration or self-congratulation, the reality of our situation pulled us back to the present, where we found ourselves dealing with any number of challenges, like Din crying, changing a diaper in the rain, or straining uphill with our heavy packs. The trail made sure that we would remain humble. Far from feeling arrogant, we were constantly left wondering if we would make it to Mexico.

11

Alms for the Poor

Trout Lake, Washington, to Cascade Locks, Oregon
July 29–August 1 60 miles

D in loved seeing all the people. It gave her a chance to
practice her newfound waving ability, greeting everyone
she could. While she mostly enjoyed the travel, she still had her
moments when she was fed up with the pack, usually near the
end of the day. Toward the end of our time in Washington, this
seemed to happen with greater frequency. One evening when
we were about two miles from camp, she started fussing, on the
verge of crying. I tried the usual tricks, singing "Wheels on the
Bus" and other songs, but to no avail. With no campsite nearby,
I dropped the pack and picked her up, then re-shouldered the
pack and continued down the trail. Any indication of tears went
away, replaced by a smile that stretched from ear to ear. She
jumped up and down in my arms, and I, too, couldn't help but
smile. Any frustration I had melted away, replaced with pure
joy. I continued down to camp with Din in my arms, alternating
between carrying her normally, holding her off to my side like a
plane hovering just inches over the plants, and then lifting her
above my head to face Alana.

The next day, the same progression began in the evening:
Din getting fussy, and me trying the tricks and then eventually
relenting to her demands to be carried. However, this time it
was a three-mile carry to camp. There was some playing again,

but the longer distance resulted in both of us being more than ready to reach camp by the last mile. Din got so much joy from being carried, which made me wish I could do so for the rest of the PCT. But it wasn't sustainable. My arms were tired, and the additional workload left me exhausted.

The fatigue sapped my patience, increasing my frustration throughout the next day. Carrying Din on my back, I quickly grew irritated with her fussiness, lacking the usual enthusiasm to sing songs or try to soothe her. To compound the challenge, Din was teething, leaving her even more irritable. Too tired to carry her in my arms, I tried carrying the pack in front, drawing curious glances from passersby. "You'll do anything to get a baby to stop crying, right," I muttered to myself. But this adjustment made no difference. Overwhelmed and out of ideas, I stopped, setting Din down in the middle of the trail and sitting off to the side. Alana came to the rescue with patience and a level head, calming Din by walking her up and down the trail while I tried to get my head straight.

Tough moments like these often left me feeling ashamed of myself and embarrassed about my behavior. Not only did I see myself as failing Alana by not being someone she could depend upon in that moment, but also as setting a poor example for Din. There were many instances on the trail that left me pondering what kind of father I wanted to be and what kind of example I wanted to put forward for Din. My limited time parenting had brought about plenty of moments of frustration and demands for patience in ways I'd never previously experienced. I didn't want to be the type of father overwhelmed by his emotions. In many ways, the PCT was the ideal proving ground, offering plenty of uncertainty and adversity to test our physical, mental, and emotional mettle. The difficulties were real, but they were no excuse for poor behavior.

Besides our worries related to diapers, one of our primary concerns for the trip was bees. Alana is severely allergic and had already experienced her fair share of anaphylactic reactions. In 2020, before we started dating, she was evacuated by a Blackhawk helicopter from deep within the Alaska Range after getting stung by a yellowjacket in the cockpit of a friend's plane—after they crashed on a primitive airstrip following an aborted takeoff. No more than two months later, she was stung again while doing forestry field work in remote Alaska. In that instance, she was able to get to services much more quickly, but her lip swelled up like a balloon. The following summer, she ordered honeybees and thought it would be prudent to go to an allergist before they arrived. The allergist found that she was allergic to every single type of bee/hornet/wasp, with the sole exception of honeybees. Needless to say, though we were well versed and prepared, encounters with bees remained a serious concern that was often top of mind.

There were numerous reports of bees throughout the last section in Washington—in particular, close to the state line near Cascade Locks, Oregon— including tales from other hikers about being stung. This left us more vigilant than usual. Late one morning, we were hiking through a closed-canopy forest when Alana screamed. Something had stung her on the back of her calf. She began to panic, and I urged her to move farther down the trail in case we were near a hive or the insect struck again. Meanwhile, I grabbed the Zyrtec from her pack and gave her a pill. She exhibited no signs of an allergic reaction beyond minor swelling at the sting area, so we decided to pick up our packs and continue walking.

Later in the day, Alana was still feeling nervous. Though
nothing had transpired from the sting, every buzzing bee that
flew by visibly agitated her, to the point that her hair stood
on end. Without knowing how severe a reaction another sting
might cause, Alana was left feeling unsettled. We looked at the
map. Come morning, we would be near a well-trafficked road,
offering us a bailout option to the town of Carson, Washington.
So it was that we opted to end our time in Washington early,
planning to skip the final thirty miles in hopes that Oregon was
home to far fewer stinging insects.

We hit the road just as a pickup with a topper rounded the
bend, heading our way. No more than two seconds passed after
we stuck out our thumbs before the truck had its turn signal
on and was slowing to a stop in a pullout across the road. What
luck! We went up to the passenger window to see if they would
give us a ride into town, but as it turned out, the truck hadn't
stopped for us. It was a couple with two of their grandkids, and
they'd pulled off to park and hike down to a waterfall, a few
miles distant. We spoke with them about our trip, and after a
few minutes the woman, Delia, insisted on forgoing the hike
and giving us a ride into town.

After pleasant conversation, Delia dropped us off at the grocery store in Carson. I sat in the shade up against the store at
the edge of the parking lot, while Alana went with Din to get
a coffee next door. An older woman came around the corner
and asked if I was going to go inside to get something. Thinking
that she was an employee about to kick me off the property,
I answered, "Yes, I'm just waiting for my wife to return. She's
grabbing a coffee over there." The woman said, "Okay," but
then just continued to stand there, so I introduced myself and
told her what we were doing. She was kind and introduced
herself as Karen, but my words seemed to go right over her head.
Again, she asked if I was going to go inside, and I answered the
same as before. Another moment passed, and she said, "I could

get you some sandwiches or snacks if you wanted something."
That's when I realized she thought I was homeless.

I politely refused her offer and said that we were just looking
for a ride. She thought on this for a few minutes, and then placed
a call to her husband, who, judging from her side of the conversation, quickly dismissed her idea of giving us a ride. Karen
disappeared into the store, soon thereafter reemerging with two
grocery bags filled to the brim. Inside each was a cornucopia of
snacks, including granola bars, muffins, fruit rollups, chicken
wraps, donuts, and more. She'd bought nearly $100 worth of
food for us. Alana, now returned with her coffee, and I didn't
know what to say, so we thanked Karen profusely. Evidently
still feeling generous, she pulled her wallet out of her purse,
extending a wad of bills. We refused, insisting again that we were
not destitute. She departed, telling us that we could find further
help at the local church.

As we were marveling at this experience and wondering what
to do with our new treasures, an old Ford Explorer swung
around in the parking lot right in front of us. The driver, with
more fingers than teeth, asked if we needed any help.

"Well, we're trying to find a ride down to Bridge of the
Gods"—the famous and picturesque steel-truss bridge spanning the Columbia River into Oregon.

"I'm going right past there—y'all are welcome to come
along."

The car was strewn with bags, tools, papers, and old fast-food
wrappers. He hurriedly threw stuff over the back seat into the
trunk, while we shouldered our packs and squeezed in. Along
the way, he told us about his battles with his fentanyl-abusing
ex-wife, how smart his kids were, and how he had turned his life
around after he stopped doing meth and smoking weed. About
halfway through the ride, Din started bawling for no reason,
and we wondered if we had made a mistake in taking him up
on the ride.

It became apparent that he too thought we were homeless. The discussion centered on his job at the local paper mill, and he asked if I wanted to work there with him. I chuckled, saying, "Nah thanks, man. I've got a job." He dropped us off on the north side of the bridge, and as I got out, fast-food cups, receipts, and wrappers flew out the door with me. While I was busy trying to pick them up, he offered me a job again and told me that he'd been where I was. He said he knew it was difficult, but that I could turn things around, just like he had. I listened politely, said thanks for the ride, and with a wave we were off.

We passed much of our gifted food to a group of other thru-hikers taking pictures in front of the Bridge of the Gods. They seemed just as confused about who we were as our two benefactors, but gladly took some muffins and fruit rollups. I snapped photos of Alana in front of the "Bridge of the Gods" sign, and then we continued across. The Columbia River roared beneath the grates. A smile began to widen across my face with Din on my back, a breeze blowing upriver, and traffic slowly passing by to the side. The fulfillment and satisfaction of what we had accomplished came over me like a wave. Sure, we had only hiked through one state. But those three weeks in Washington were proof enough that what we were doing was possible, and that the only thing that could stop us would be ourselves. Or flying, stinging things.

PUNCHBOWL FALLS

SKOONICHUK FALLS

TWISTER FALLS

TUNNEL FALLS

YELLOW JACKET

THUNDER STORMS

PORTLAND

CASCADE LOCKS
TIMBERLINE LODGE
OLALLIE LAKE RESORT

SALEM

BIG LAKE YOUTH CAMP

SISTERS

SHELTER COVE

CRATER LAKE

ASHLAND

HUCKLEBERRIES

BIG FOREST

CRATER LAKE

OREGON

12

Into Oregon

Cascade Locks to Timberline Lodge, Oregon
Timberline Lodge to Olallie Lake, Oregon
Sisters to Shelter Cove Resort, Oregon
August 2–August 13 174 miles

S topping early in Washington ended up being a much-needed respite from our relentless pace. Since the outset, we hadn't taken any days off, hiking an average of twenty miles a day in an effort to get south as quickly as possible. It was only the first of August, but the Sierras loomed ahead, and any dillydallying increased the risk of running into snow later. If we wanted to finish the PCT, we had to keep moving. But the combination of poor sleep, heavy packs, and inadequate recovery had taken its toll, pushing us into exhaustion. In Cascade Locks, we staggered into a hotel room midday and proceeded to spend most of the day in bed. My legs felt like lead, and the lightest of efforts would leave me looking for the nearest place to sit down. We grabbed some ice cream across the street, and then wandered over to a park by the Columbia River. Despite going no more than a quarter mile, I found myself utterly spent carrying Din back to the hotel, and was more than ready to collapse into bed. It was clear that we'd needed the rest.

The next day we walked along the bike path that ran parallel to the highway toward the Eagle Creek trailhead, gorging ourselves on the blackberries that lined the trail. I'd pick a few berries for myself, and then hand them back to Din over my shoulder. She'd eagerly grab them, cramming them in her mouth, staining her hands, lips, and cheeks with the purple juice. Alana and I couldn't help but laugh as Din continued to reach out with her little hand to ask for more.

Din wasn't shy about eating, whether it was breastfeeding or sharing our food. If it was edible, she was content. Alana liked to say that Din was stealing from her twice: sapping her energy through breastfeeding and nibbling on our daily snack supply. It seemed like a joke at first, but each day this tiny human would enjoy a surprising amount of the snacks that we had packed for Alana and me. At night, Din would happily eat as much of our dinner as we gave her, crawling on top of us to reach our spoons and reaching for the pot to snag the contents within, especially if they were mashed potatoes.

After hiking up and down what seemed like countless mountain passes in Washington, we were looking forward to Oregon, with its fabled flat terrain. Oregon boasts far less elevation change than any other region of the PCT, inspiring some hikers to take on various self-imposed challenges like the 2-week challenge (hiking the 495 miles of trail in Oregon in 2 weeks) or the 24-hour challenge (hiking as many miles as possible within 24 hours).

In no position to participate in such feats of extreme athleticism, we contented ourselves with upping our daily mileage goal, from the 20 miles per day we'd averaged in Washington to 22.5 miles. Our hope was that the flatter terrain would offer us a chance to finally recover and have more time to ourselves, while still making miles. We envisioned more relaxed evenings at camp and the freedom to embark on side adventures, instead of feeling bound by a rigid schedule, needing to maintain forward progress at all costs.

It didn't take us long to realize that while Oregon might be flatter than other regions overall, it doesn't mean that it's *flat*. We built an image of plainlike terrain, with only slight rises and dips for miles and miles. That image was shattered early on, as hiking the first section of trail through this gentler stretch of the Cascades still led us up steep 2,500-foot climbs, down and then up another. The additional hills were a morale killer. I hadn't fully recovered from hitting the red zone at the end of Washington, and the undulating terrain did us no favors. Nonetheless, we still managed to reach our mileage goals each day, collapsing into the tent early each night utterly exhausted.

Following our third night in Oregon, camped just outside the iconic Timberline Lodge, we woke to strong winds and low clouds blanketing Mount Hood. The wind intensified as we went down the trail, whipping up sand from the river below and blowing it over the path. Dirt blew into my eyes, and Din, despite her exhaustion, struggled to get any sleep. Fortunately, it didn't take long to get into the shelter of the forest. There, we finally discovered the flatness that Oregon is known for. The trail, much gentler than we were accustomed to, wound through closed-canopy pine forests with open understories. The absence of shrubs allowed for expansive views on either side of the trail, which, when combined with the flatter terrain, made for a notably pleasant stroll.

Until Oregon, one of our biggest problems on the trail had been Din's naps. Generally, she had no problem falling asleep in the carrier; it was her staying asleep that was the issue. We had experienced the most difficulty with other hikers. We'd try to pass by silently, waving and mouthing hi, all while trying to indicate the sleeping load on our back. Still, the other hikers, oblivious, would not only greet us as usual but might comment, loudly, "Is that a baby in there?!" or, "Oh, isn't she cute!" or, "Aw, look at the little guy taking a nap," jolting Din awake. After having spent up to forty-five minutes on some occasions trying to soothe her to sleep, we saw the disruptions as frustrating, leaving us wanting to bang our heads against a wall.

Exasperated, we finally came upon a solution. When Din was sleeping, whoever wasn't carrying her would take the lead, warning others who passed, "Hi, we have a sleeping baby back there." This often elicited some confused looks, especially in the instances when the lookout was well ahead of the parent carrying Din, with no baby in sight. Some of the time there'd be a big group talking or we were separated, leaving us to resort to sign language. We'd wave our hands madly in the air to get their attention, then with a smile bring a solo raised finger to our mouths while trying to also sign that a baby was sleeping. I'm sure we looked quite the sight.

This strategy worked 95 percent of the time, allowing us to hike down the trail with significantly less worry that others would wake Din. The number of anxiety-ridden miles decreased, with us no longer craning our necks around each bend, desperately hoping that there'd be nobody passing us so that Din could continue with her nap. With her sleeping more during the day, it bade well for her sleeping more at night. And, as a result, us sleeping more as well. If all our hijinks and tricks proved to be a failure, our last resort was to use the cardboard sign that Alana had made in Cascade Locks that read: "Plz let baby sleep. Thx!"

We almost always hiked within sight of each other, but there were times, such as if one of us was getting water, going to the bathroom, or washing diapers, when we would hike separately for short durations. So it wasn't unusual when, one afternoon as we hiked through the Warm Springs Reservation, Alana told me she was going to stop to go to the bathroom and that Din and I could carry on.

It was midafternoon, and we had already done twenty miles on the day, with hopes of reaching twenty-five, our biggest day of the trip so far. We were making decent time, so without any real sense of urgency, Din and I ambled on up a hill. I stopped at the numerous huckleberry bushes along the way, picking some for myself and handing some back to Din. We continued this way for a couple miles or so, and at the top I debated sitting down to wait for Alana. We had been going slow and stopping often; I figured she was likely close behind and decided just to mosey on.

A few minutes after dropping down the other side, I thought I heard someone yelling. When I heard it again, I paused to listen to which direction it was coming from. Nothing for a moment, then a whistle pierced the air behind me. Immediately, I turned and ran back up the trail. A minute later, I found Alana coming my way in tears and hyperventilating. A yellowjacket had gotten caught between the tongue of her shoe and her foot, stinging her. She had already broken out into hives around her neck and waist, and was starting to panic.

"It's okay. It's okay. I'm here now. We have medicine. Breathe," I reassured her.

I had Alana sit down on the side of the trail while I took off my pack to grab the Zyrtec and the EpiPen. Din was crying, wanting to be close to mom and due for a feeding and diaper change. Alana took 7.5 mg of Zyrtec, and I lifted Din out from her carrier. We talked over the situation and what we could do while we waited for the medicine to kick in. Olallie Lake Resort, five miles ahead on the trail, seemed like our best option for the night if we could make it there. In the meantime, two hikers approached from different directions. I explained what was going on and asked if they had any Benadryl, in hopes of finding a stronger treatment. One did, and I quickly gave it to Alana while the other hiker looked on.

Alana said she was feeling better and thought she could hike to the resort, when all of a sudden, she said, "I'm going to need the epi."

"Okay do you want me to do it or do you—oh shit!" I watched as her eyes rolled back in her head and she fell back to the slope behind her. "Alana, Alana, stay with me," I said. With Din crying in one arm, I took the cover off the needle with the other and jabbed it into her thigh.

I put Din down on the trail and grabbed the inReach off my pack. Finagling the cover off, I hit the SOS button. "Alana, can you hear me? Stay with me," I said. We were in an open forest, but the device didn't seem to connect to any satellites, and I watched as the message status spun in circles, indicating that it remained unsent. One of the hikers, Joe, offered to go to a nearby high point and was able to get the message through from there. I dictated messages to him, so that emergency services had the clearest possible picture of our situation.

Alana's condition was rapidly deteriorating, and she kept going in and out of consciousness. She nodded that she could hear me but whispered that she was unable to see. The shock progressed further, and she soon started shivering. Din sat crying on the trail as I frantically rummaged through our pack for our sleeping quilt, finding it buried beneath our food and clothes, using it to cover Alana after putting one of our sleeping pads underneath her. Besides tending to Alana and communicating with emergency services, I had my hands full with Din, who seemed to want nothing but mom. I was able to distract her for short periods by giving her jerky and cheese, but otherwise she refused to be put down. Amidst the chaos, Alana said she was feeling nauseous, a symptom we later learned indicates the body's last efforts to rid itself of toxins before giving in.

We finally received word that emergency response was on the way but had no answer regarding their timing or method of arrival. Without any further recourse for immediate treatment, my hands were tied, our circumstances left to fate. The necessity of caring for Din in addition to Alana kept me grounded and my head from spinning. Still, I was left worrying about *ifs*. *If* the medicine Alana had already taken would work quickly enough in her body to stave off the worst; *if* emergency response would arrive in time; *if* I'd be able to keep Din content on my own for much longer; *if* these were the last moments we might spend together as a family. The hives weren't getting any worse, and after another twenty minutes, Alana had regained her vision. She remained conscious, and shortly thereafter more hikers arrived, including a nurse practitioner, Martina, and her son, who happened to have more EpiPens and the steroid prednisone, which she administered to Alana.

With Alana trending better, help on the way, and more experienced hands around to help, I was able to put my efforts elsewhere. I focused on Din, who had become somewhat consolable with the improvement of her mom's symptoms. We received word that emergency response would be arriving by ground, and Alana felt up for hiking out to meet them. I grabbed our packs—the baby carrier on my back and our gear pack strapped across my front—and Alana shakily led the way as Martina and her son accompanied us for the three-mile trek to the road.[1] Still in need of a diaper change, Din started to cry again, at this point wanting absolutely nothing but mom. I stopped to finally change her diaper and give her more jerky, telling the others to continue. Both seemed to improve things

---

1. They were beyond kind to do so, changing their own hiking plans in order to help us.

for the time being and we hopped back on the trail, walking briskly to catch up to the others.

About an hour and a half later, we reached the road, finding only an older couple with their son out to watch the sunset. They had seen an ambulance pass by a little while earlier, but it had returned going back the other direction. We assumed this was the emergency-response team trying to find us. Communicating via satellite was frustrating, since everything on both ends happened on a delay. Minutes later, I received a new message saying that the first responders were hiking in on a different trailhead, with the idea of cutting us off at an intersection on the trail we'd passed over a mile ago. I reiterated that we were already at the road, and we decided to sit tight, staying in a known location to avoid further confusion.

The sight of us with our packs and the baby had piqued the curiosity of the older couple, and they began peppering us with questions—"Are you doing the whole trail?" and, "Even with the baby?"—even as I explained our somewhat-dire circumstances and that we were waiting for emergency services. The information seemed to go in one ear and out the other, and the couple kept rapid-firing questions. They eventually stepped away, only to return with marshmallows and graham crackers, offering us the lot. About that time, a fire truck pulled up, followed by the ambulance and the sheriff. The couple lingered, still asking questions, before I politely told them that we needed to talk with the emergency personnel.

The paramedics quickly cleared Alana, determining that she had recovered and there was no immediate cause for concern, forcing us to figure out what we wanted to do next. After going over what had happened, I spoke with the lead paramedic and sheriffs at length about our options. The lead paramedic gave me the lay of the land, explaining the distances to all the nearest towns, what medical facilities each had, and how easy it was to get to them. "Unfortunately, I can't give you an EpiPen, but I'd definitely recommend getting another one before continuing on again," he said. Ahead was the resort, which was connected to the road but without any real services. Beyond was no man's land, as far as emergency personnel was concerned, where the roads ended and any medical emergency would likely require a helicopter. The nearest town with medical facilities was about an hour and a half's drive away, and if we went there, the paramedic figured we might as well go to Salem, a half-hour beyond but with more comprehensive services.

It didn't seem wise to continue without additional EpiPens, but it also felt as if our hands were tied. Due to bureaucratic delays, Alana was without healthcare for the year. Both of us had heard the horror stories of people getting charged $10,000-plus for an ambulance ride and we wanted no part of that, especially out-of-pocket.

I spoke with Alana, filling her in on our options, and we agreed that we wanted to go to town, but did not want to take the ambulance. I mentioned that to the paramedic, who said he'd see what he could do.

"So these guys need to get an EpiPen, but I can't just drop one from the ambulance on the side of the trail..." he told the sheriff as they stood off to the side.

The sheriff responded with a laugh and asked, "What do you want me to do?"

After more discussion, the paramedic approached me, saying, "Well, since we are going that way [into town] anyways, we can give you guys a courtesy ride in the back of the ambulance."

We took him up on his offer, piling into the ambulance immediately, before he changed his mind. The back doors shut and off we went, along bumpy forest roads, onto county roads, and finally State Highway 22. Martina, along with the paramedics, had told us that Alana shouldn't breastfeed for twenty-four hours after having taken the prednisone, so we tried, without much success, to feed Din regular food. She wailed away, hungry and uncomfortable, until finally we reached cell service and found that the advice about prednisone wasn't true and that Alana could breastfeed after all. The ambulance sped along into the night, finally reaching the lights of Stayton, the nearest town with medical services, close to 10 p.m. after an hour and a half of travel. Din had fallen fast asleep in the ambulance and remained undisturbed as we carried her into the only hotel in town, content and with her belly full of milk.

Even though our break from the trail was due to unpleasant circumstances, we wholeheartedly welcomed the time off, relaxing in the luxury of Central Oregon's finest two-star hotels. After over a month of running ourselves ragged, we took not one but two full days off, catching up on sleep and stuffing ourselves with town food. We were able to obtain a prescription from Alana's allergist back home, picking up four more EpiPens at a pharmacy in nearby Salem. After buying more antihistamine pills, we returned to the trail with what seemed like (and what we hoped would be) a multi-year medical supply.

Despite the circumstances, Alana still wished to continue on the PCT, with the caveat that another sting would mean the end of our trip. There was no argument from me—the PCT wasn't worth dying over, and we could only hope that the bees and wasps farther south were friendlier, having weathered two stings already, only a quarter of the way along our journey.

After getting everything we needed in Salem, we took a bus to Sisters, the closest and logistically easiest option for rejoining the trail. We spent a night at the town campground, playing cards for the first time on the trip, savoring a rare moment of free time. In the morning, we picked up socks to replace the ones full of holes that I'd been wearing and stopped at the local bakery before finding a ride back to the trail. This was our second time having skipped a section,[2] and it felt strange to resume at a different point. However, in the grand scheme of things, the distances we'd missed weren't terribly long, and the terrain was likely similar to what we had previously traversed through and were about to encounter again. In other words, we weren't missing much, plus the idea of hitchhiking thirty miles on rough, remote forest-service roads to return to the exact spot where the ambulance had picked us up didn't seem essential to fulfilling our vision, which was to have an immersive outdoor experience as a family and not log every last foot on the PCT.

After lunch and sorting our resupply boxes at Big Lake Youth Camp, a Christian summer camp next to the trail outside Sisters, we set forth once more. We walked forward with some hesitation, as the sun was shining brightly overhead and we were entering an old burn area, which was devoid of water for nearly twenty miles. The faint smell of smoke from fires to the west lingered as we hiked alongside downed trees and standing snags, leafless and stripped of their bark. The terrain underfoot changed as well, dirt giving way to volcanic rock, which slowed us with less stable footing. Before reaching the highway at McKenzie Pass, just southwest of Sisters, we crossed a dirt road, where we found gallons of water that someone had kindly cached for hikers. With the unexpected water, we stopped earlier than planned to set up camp. The wind blew strong until we turned in at twilight. The sky softly lit up with color before turning a vibrant golden, orange, and pink at the horizon.

By morning, the light smoke that had hung in the air the day before had thickened. Out toward the west, a dense cloud of smoke hovered, enshrouding everything around it. The same appeared to be true at lower elevations to the east. Behind us

2. This time fifty-seven miles.

to the north we could still see Mount Washington nearly ten miles distant, and while the air to the south was hazy, the smoke wasn't very thick. From the very beginning, we'd decided that there was nothing that we'd do or push through if it meant deliberately endangering our baby. If we had to skip a section as a result, so be it. Risking Din's health wasn't worth doing every single step of the trail. With this in mind, we wondered if the smoke was too much and whether it was worth skipping ahead to clearer air, free of the particulate matter that's so harmful to little (and big) lungs.

About a hundred yards up the road stood a stone observatory, used by local groups in Sisters and Bend to stargaze. I ran up the steps, gazing out on the landscape below. I could see the volcanic rocks we'd crossed the day before, as well as portions of the Three Sisters, the volcanic peaks standing tall amidst the haze. With cell phone in hand, I wandered around the top, searching for a signal. I was able to find just enough bars to check the air-quality index (AQI) throughout the state as well as wind and smoke forecasts for the coming days. It turns out that babies follow the same guidelines as adults when it comes to air pollution. Anything over 150 AQI was deemed hazardous for both groups, and in such conditions, it's recommended to limit any extended outdoor activity. While I couldn't find any readings for our exact location, the AQI in the nearby, very smoky areas was just past the 150 mark. Alana and I talked it over. The air around us was relatively clear, plus the forecast seemed favorable going forward. We'd be hiking in smoke, but we felt comfortable taking the risk that it wouldn't be too damaging.

Meanwhile, a mother and her two kids had made their way up the stairs and joined me at the top. They admired the view for a few minutes and then started talking about the PCT, figuring that it had to pass nearby. I pointed out Mount Washington, and then showed them the path through the volcanic rocks and where the trail crossed the road below the Three Sisters.

The woman asked, "Are you hiking it?"'

"Yes, my wife, daughter, and I are. We started near Canada and are trying to make it to Mexico."

"How long have you been walking?"

"Well, we started July 8th, so I figure that's about five weeks now."

The little boy's eyes lit up, growing wide. He exclaimed, "With no sleep?!"

I chuckled and reassured him that we slept every night[3] and that we had a tent and sleeping bags. This prompted him to ask, "Do you have a house?" I laughed again and said yes, explaining that we were out by choice and for fun. We weren't homeless.

The smoke around us came from a wildfire about thirty miles to the south. Risk of wildfire had again become a regular concern on the trail, as fires regularly blazed from Northern California to the Canadian border. After decades of forest mismanagement in the West that resulted in fires being put out as quickly as possible, the forests had accumulated abundant fuel in the understory, making them ripe for far larger and deadlier fires. And that's exactly what was happening. In 2020, California had its largest fire complex on record. The August Complex burned throughout the state, consuming over one million acres. The following year it happened again. The Dixie Fire, California's largest single fire on record (963,309 acres), tore through the state's northern forests, destroying communities, homes, and animal habitat.

While we hiked through the burn areas, we sometimes came across other hikers who lamented the destruction and its impact on the ecosystem. But the reality in many of these cases was far

---

3. If you could call it sleep. His question was more on point than I'd like to admit.

different. Perhaps counterintuitively, a mature forest offers the least use for all animals, humans included. Outside of logging, there isn't much that mature stands can provide. The large trees shade out the understory, resulting in minimal growth for smaller trees, shrubs, forbs, and grasses. Fire is a natural cycle within the ecosystem, resetting the system and forcing the start of ecological succession, a process that improves the soil health and fosters new growth. After a fire, grasses and flowers emerge first, growing as early as the following year among the burnt remains and ashen ground. This new growth attracts wildlife like deer and birds, which are in turn followed by shrubs and the first round of saplings. The area continues to grow over the years as the plants compete, eventually returning to a mature forest.

Certain moments on the trail reminded me of a story from the book *Kabloona*, which details the fifteen months the French adventurer Gontran de Poncins spent living with the Inuit in the Canadian Arctic in the late 1930s. The author quickly discovered the many cultural differences, a distinction defined by one event during a hunting trip with a group of Inuit. After traveling with the group for multiple days from the village, de Poncins was looking forward to getting back before a storm arrived. Yet the group had different ideas. A few miles away, they decided to stop their dog teams, start making tea, and set up camp for a night or two. The author stomped and howled. Town was right there! They could basically see it! They could beat the storm! Why didn't they just continue? But the Inuit were content to just be where they were, not obsessed with some destination or goal.

The West is explicitly results-, destination-, and goal-oriented, and the trail mindset often serves as an extension of this. Questions like "How many miles to the next water source? The next camp? The next resupply?" can create a sense of urgency, in which one is focused on some future destination rather than the present moment.

Babies, however, have the gift of not yet being indoctrinated by the dominant culture. So with that, Din served as an antidote to our often destination-oriented and frantic ways. One day in Oregon we had a long water carry, needing to travel 19.5 miles between sources. The day was hot and much of it was spent in a recent burn, so we wanted to move quickly to avoid dehydration. But Din had other ideas, fussing in the pack for a couple of miles and refusing to be consoled by the usual jerky, rock, or medley of songs. We decided to stop in a rare spot of shade beneath a small stand of live trees to see if she wanted to sleep. She didn't, so instead we played for an hour, mimicking each other's sounds and throwing around broken pine branches. Under similar circumstances on a different day, we hiked off-trail to a nearby lake and splashed away in the shallows, Din just as happy as could be. Refreshed, we carried on—just 30 minutes later, after only a slight delay. Neither moment required us to forge on at some hellish pace, and in fact we easily made up the "lost" time. By stopping and focusing on the present, we had found joy. At least for the moment, we had found enough.

I would have loved to include color photos within the book, but printing costs were exorbitant and impractical. If you are interested in seeing the following pictures in color, please scan the QR code above, which will take you to my website. I have also uploaded many more photos there. If you'd prefer to enter the site URL manually, go to animaltreks.com/PCTphotos

Din taking a nap during a break on one of our first few days on trail.

Din playing with rocks during a water break.

We were awed by the massive trees in the Glacier Peak Wilderness.

Din waving from camp.

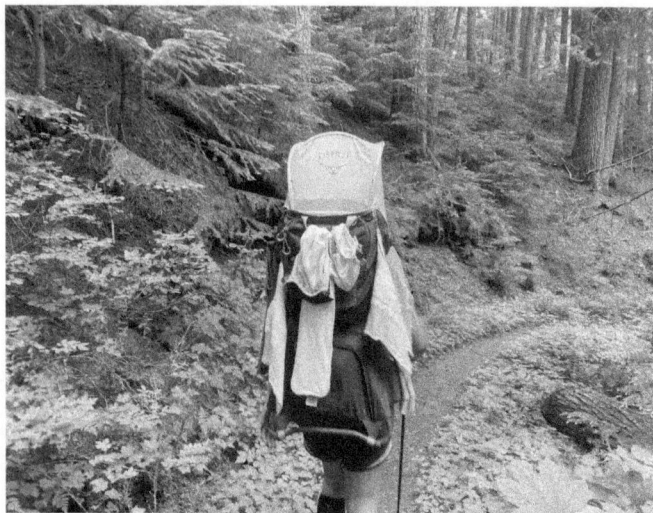

The Diaper Brigade: We almost always had diapers hanging off our packs to dry.

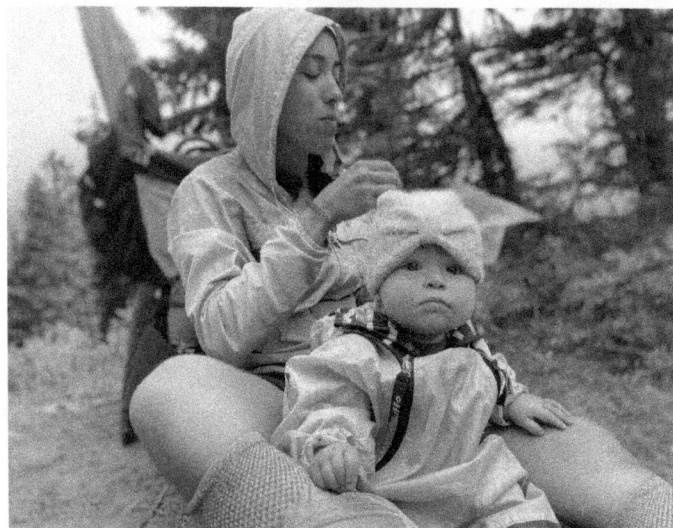

Bundled up on a cold, wet day in Mount Rainier National Park.

Dad carrying Din the last few miles one evening to camp.

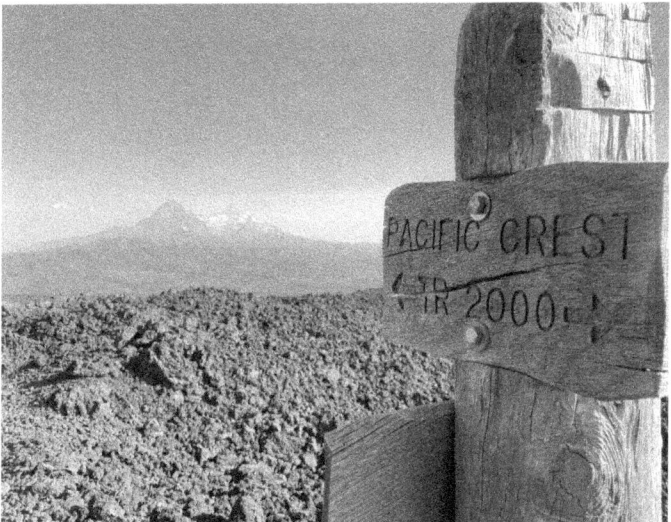

Oregon brought lava rock fields, like this one on a smoky day near the peaks of the Three Sisters.

*The Cedar Creek Fire tore through the trail in Central Oregon,
leaving little shade and us concerned about overexposing Din.*

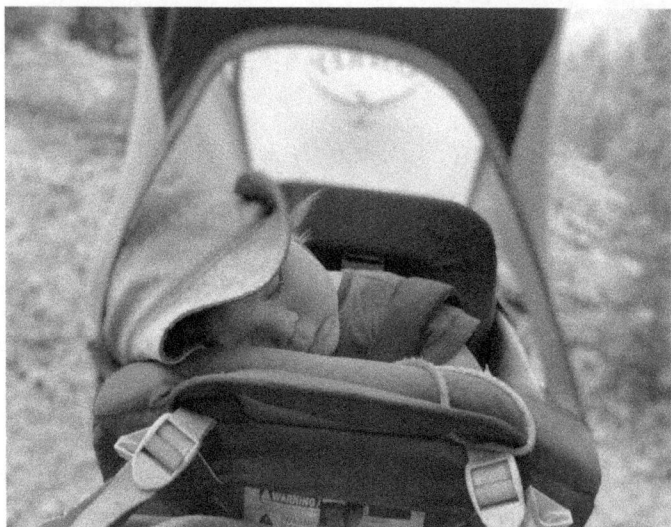

All of us were often tired. Some of us got to nap more than others.

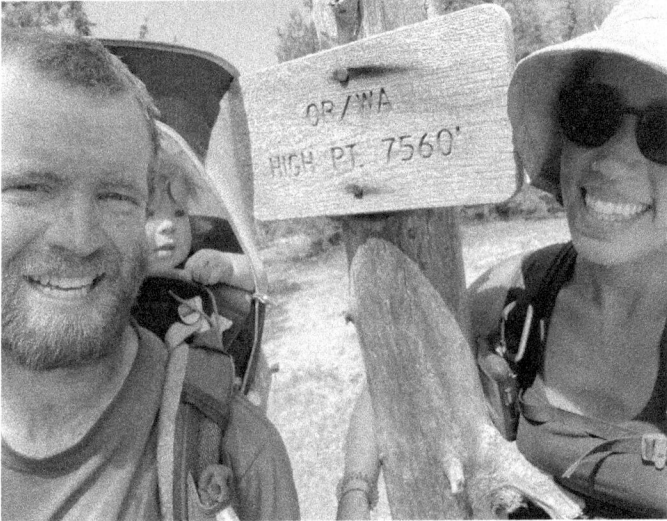

A rare shot of us as a family, north of Crater Lake.

Din loved to explore, crawling around whenever she could on breaks and at camp.

We were rewarded with majestic views of Mount Shasta after a hot day on Hat Creek Rim.

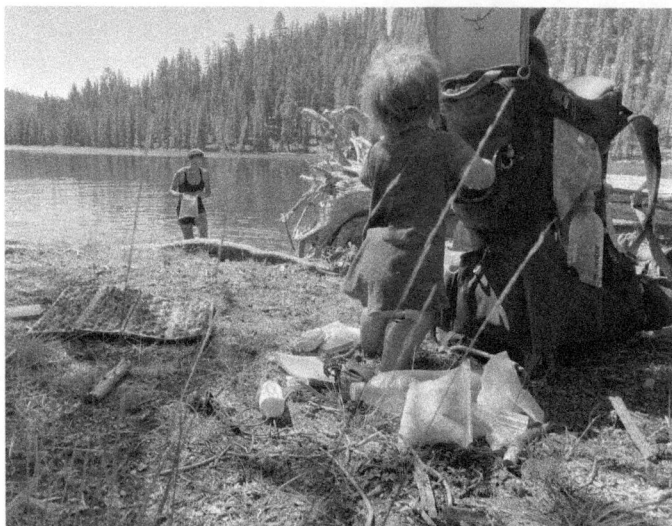

Din causing chaos on a break in Northern California.

Alana and Din crossing a stream via a downed tree in Northern California.

Alana and Din crossing a stream in Northern California.

Alana admiring the alpenglow just north of Sierra City.

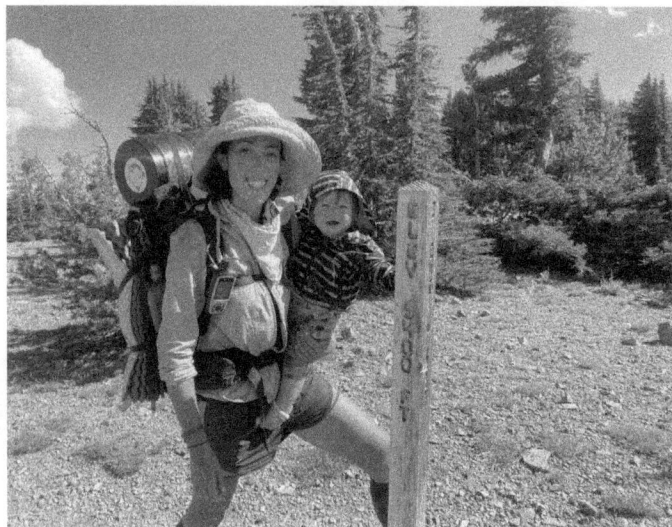

All smiles atop Dick's Pass at 9,400 feet.

Din was the only one excited about us carrying a bear can.

It was a struggle to figure out a good way to attach the second bear can.

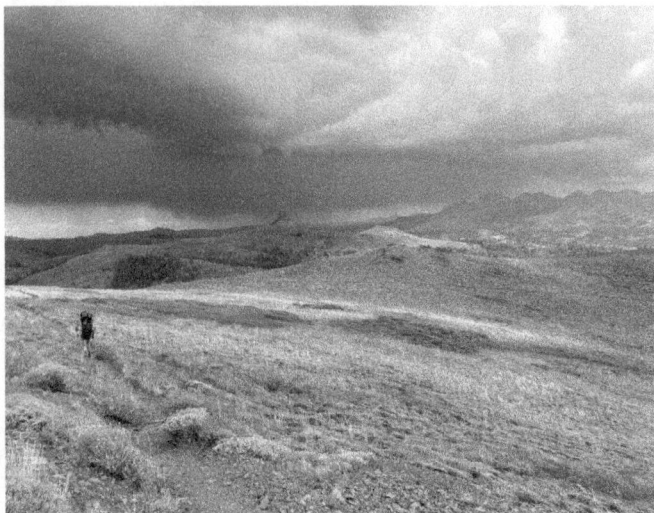

Afternoon storms became a regular occurrence as we approached the heart of the Sierras.

Adam hikes ahead of the author in the High Sierra.

13

Where There's Smoke...

Shelter Cove to Crater Lake, Oregon
August 14–August 17 69 miles

W e were never planning on stopping long at Shelter Cove, a resort and marina on Oregon's Odell Lake—just staying long enough to collect our resupply box, sort our gear, and continue. I stepped inside the store, telling the manager behind the desk that I was a PCT thru-hiker looking to pick up a resupply box. He pulled out a book and started running his finger down a list of names, some highlighted, marking hikers who had already passed through and picked up their boxes. But he didn't see us on there.

"What's your name again?" he asked.

"Jack McClure, it might also be under my wife's name, Alana."

He searched again, looking even further back. But, like before, no luck. I asked if I could try looking and he passed the book over the counter. I scanned the pages. Sure enough, our names were not there. He invited me into the back room where they kept the boxes, but nothing was to be found. Where was our box? It had been sent nearly two weeks earlier. We called our friend who was sending our boxes from home to get the tracking number, but she was out of state, visiting family until the following morning. What would we do without the box? We could probably scrounge for food, but without our supplies, we wouldn't have diaper stuff for Din. Without any other options, we set up our tent and waited.

Later that afternoon, I watched the UPS driver unload boxes from his truck. Still no sign of ours. We figured we might as well take advantage of the situation, going for a swim in the lake and doing laundry. We were delighted to find some trail friends of ours, like Adam, whom we'd met in Southern Washington, hanging around as well. In the last resupply box, I'd been shipped a new pair of trail shoes. Though they were the same size as the previous pair, the new ones were inexplicably tearing my feet apart and I'd hobbled into the resort with numerous hotspots and some small blisters. Adam was kind enough to share some Leukotape, which upon application provided instant relief.

By morning, we got the tracking numbers from our friend, learning that, for whatever reason, the boxes were still in transit and were days from arriving. Neither of us felt like we could afford to wait that long, so we decided to come up with a plan B. The resort had a store, but its offerings were limited and expensive. Alana discovered a gas station ten miles away with a broader selection, including diapers. If we could find a way there, we could probably resupply.

In the meantime, we would keep an eye on the "hiker box." At each resupply point, there are often a few cardboard boxes where hikers can deposit unused or unwanted items—typically food and gear. Oftentimes, it's not anything that's very appetizing or useful: unmarked Ziploc bags of mystery powder, half-filled Ziplocs of rice and beans, extra accessories for water filters.... Luckily for us, for whatever reason, almost all the dozen or so hikers at Shelter Cove had received excess food in their resupply boxes, all of which they'd donated to the hiker box. Quickly, we scored high-end snacks like peanut butter M&Ms

and cashews, as well as curry dinners, cous cous, energy bars, nut mixes, and cookies. Once people found out we were looking for food, they began giving us stuff directly. Before we even went to the gas station, we had gathered about 85 percent of the food we needed for the next section.

The manager of the resort was kind enough to arrange a ride for me to the gas station with a staff member, sparing me from hitchhiking or walking additional miles. There, I picked up diapers, jerky, and Clif bars, rounding out our supplies.

The next day, before we even started walking again, we were already burning up. The mid-August day was hot, the type of heat where you sweat just sitting around. From Shelter Cove, we decided to take the alternate route. Throughout the PCT, certain segments could be bypassed in favor of an alternative, whether for safety reasons, more-scenic views, or something else. Here, promises from others of fewer bugs, more water, shorter miles, and 1,800 fewer feet of elevation gain were hard to pass up—when you're hiking 2,650 miles, it's hard not to take any opportunity to shorten the distance. The trail went south to Diamond Lake, a broad, shallow lake settled in the forest, before linking back up with the official PCT about 20 miles later. This "bypass" seemed to be the unofficial main trail, as we didn't hear of anyone going via the traditional route. The route took us up alongside a clear, running creek. It was the first time since Northern Washington weeks earlier that we'd hiked parallel to running water. After leaving late in the afternoon, we were only planning to go five miles, and then camp near Diamond Lake.

We arrived within two hours, finding a serene spot nestled in the trees, not far from the lake. I took a stroll down to the water, stepping onto a mostly submerged rock just offshore and looking out over the water and surrounding forest. The pine trees were very thin, and the setting reminded me of the thin spruce trees and shallow lakes back home in Interior Alaska.

The sky directly above us was blue, but there seemed to be some type of haze on the far side of the lake. Could it be smoke? I had just checked for new fires before we left and hadn't seen reports of anything nearby. The wind was calm, without even the slightest breeze. Yet within ten minutes, the lake and forest were enshrouded in what was indeed smoke.

Alana and I mused about whether it was smart to camp there, even if no new fires had been reported. There was a campground at Crescent Lake connected to the road, six miles farther along. If we could make it there, we could hopefully find better air quality and would at least be well positioned to evacuate if worst came to worst. Still, it was already past 6 p.m. and we were reluctant to leave, not excited about getting back on the trail and getting to camp late. But we didn't have any good arguments for staying. So after Alana fed Din, we threw the packs over our shoulders and set off.

We left heading downhill at a good clip, singing to Din along the way. Halfway to the lake, Alana stopped for a bathroom break. Not more than ten minutes later, she stopped to go again. Din and I waited, playing with some leaves on a nearby tree. Alana returned frustrated and upset, saying that her foot hurt. To compound matters, she was worried she had giardia, an intestinal infection caused by a parasite found in untreated water sources. She had mentioned going multiple times earlier in the day and was concerned that she had picked up a bug somewhere. Blood in her stool didn't provide any reassurances.

I told her to take some Imodium, and then started asking clarifying questions, to figure out where she'd picked up the illness in hopes of finding a solution.

"You mentioned that you thought you had it earlier—were your other times runny and bloody like this one?"

She fired back quickly with, "What did I just tell you?"

And just like that, it erupted into something more than a discussion.

"I'm just trying to figure out when it started."

"And I told you, you're just asking stupid questions, and I'm answering them."

"You know, you're unbelievable sometimes."

"I'm answering your questions. Maybe if you weren't an asshole who wanted a robot for a wife and someone to say only what you want to hear, it'd be easier."

The conversation had taken a sharp turn, an abrupt change that caught me by surprise. Just a couple hours ago we had finished a pleasant walk to what we thought was our camp. Now, less than six miles down the trail, we were engaging in an increasingly heated argument. I immediately tried to de-escalate the situation, while also (perhaps foolishly) trying to defend myself.

"I don't tell you what to say," I said. "I just ask to be respected, not called names, and not have a wedge driven into every crack in the relationship."

She stormed off, leaving Din and I alone on the trail. I yelled after her, "Alana, come on! Can't we just talk about this?"

A mile or so later, we got to the campground and I set up camp. Alana spent almost all evening sitting off to the side on a log, not interacting with either of us or eating dinner, just looking at something on her phone. After finishing dinner, Din and I went inside the tent, off to bed. There was no further discussion between Alana and I, but I knew that this was far from over and that there would probably be fireworks the next day.

Not much had changed come morning. I didn't end up sleeping much, and Din decided to wake up early. Alana left the tent to make breakfast, while I got Din ready and began packing up. I took advantage of a nearby water spigot to wash diapers before we left to rejoin the trail.

All set and ready to go, I'd started walking through the woods back to the PCT when I heard an annoyed "Hellooo,"—Alana calling me back to see if I wanted to look at fire news on her phone.

"You don't have to call me like that."

She chuckled, and then said, "How was I supposed to get your attention?"

"You don't talk to anyone else like that."

We looked at the fire map and quibbled over small details regarding the date of a fire to the north. I said it had happened two weeks ago, and Alana said no, August 5th, ten days ago.

Reassured by our discovery of no new fires nearby, we set out again, bushwhacking back through the trees and over the logs to the trail. Less than a hundred yards later, Din started fussing in her pack and seemed on the verge of crying. Out front, I couldn't hear Alana behind me trying to sing or calm Din down, and I took that as a bad sign, bracing for the worst. Sure enough, a few moments later, Alana said, "That's it. I'm done with the trail. I'm tired of suffering."

I look back to see her storming back toward the road. "Alana!" I yelled, running the fifty yards back to catch her. I touched her shoulder, and she shoved me off, saying, "Don't touch me!"

I didn't press further on that, walking alongside her. "What do you mean? Where are you going?" I asked.

"I'm going to catch a bus at the gas station— I had Kayla [Alana's best friend] check the schedule last night. You can do whatever you want."

"So you're leaving me?"

"Yes."

My mind raced. After our initial arguments on the trail, I'd contemplated how if things went awry, we could be ending our trip early, but I never envisioned a scenario in which we would not only be leaving the trail, but doing so heading in separate directions. I dreaded the thought of losing my family, finally realizing the seriousness of our predicament.

"I don't feel this is an appropriate response, and it's an extreme escalation from yesterday. I'd like to talk this over with you."

"There's no talking. You just want to be a dictator, and have me be your robot and say whatever you want me to say and do."

"That's not true. I don't think it's appropriate to jump from where we were to leaving. This all seems impulsive and not really the way we make big decisions as a family. Can we please talk this over?"

"I'm not leaving you. I'm just done doing this—this isn't fun or enjoyable."

"Well, that's what you just said."

Meanwhile, we were walking in circles on the loop road around the campground, passing its only other occupants, a pair of women and their horses, all four of whom looked on curiously at our predicament.

"How the fuck do you get out of here?!"

"It's a loop."

"Goddamnit!"

"Can we please talk this over? You talk about me shutting down and not talking, and that's what you're doing now. If we go on the bus, where are we going?"

"WE are not going anywhere. I don't want to be around you." Alana snapped.

"So you ARE leaving me, then?"

"I suppose so."

"I really don't think that's an appropriate response," I said, falling back on the same reply I'd used earlier. "So what are we going to do from here? You're going to leave and go somewhere and just not answer my texts or calls? Can we please just sit and talk?"

"Fine, but Din needs to take a nap."

We stopped at a camp spot, setting our packs down on a picnic table. I wandered off with Din, singing her to sleep and laying her down on one of our sleeping pads spread out amidst the pines. Back at the table, there was a silence as each of us waited to see if the other had something they wanted to say. I fidgeted with a few splinters from the weathered wood, breaking them in my fingers. The blaring and jumping of my thoughts inside my head contrasted sharply with the quiet campground that surrounded us. Alana broke the silence after a couple minutes, asking how I wanted to go about resolving our issues. With a lack of clarity and no real answers, I asked if she had any ideas. She thought it would be best if we laid all our grievances on the table.

She went first, saying that I upheld a double standard, believing myself to be smarter than her, and that she didn't think I listened—issues we'd been dealing with throughout our relationship. I tried to focus on what she was saying without thinking of some type of defense or response. After years of expending what I thought was a significant amount of effort at self-improvement—through reading, journaling, and self-reflection—I was learning that my efforts were still for naught. Despite my intentions, our dynamic had foundered once again, leaving me to wonder if it was just me at fault or if the trail was a factor as well.

After she finished, I proceeded with what had been bothering me, saying I didn't feel respected or appreciated—and in fact felt taken for granted. Tears started to come out as I was explaining how I didn't feel like I could do enough, despite my constant efforts to try to make things easier for her and Din. Alana moved over to my side of the table, sitting in my lap and hugging me as I broke down sobbing.

After I regained my composure, she returned to the other side of the table, and we schemed about how we could resolve our issues. For the time being, we settled on sharing three things we were grateful for at the end of each day along with a nightly check-in, with a reevaluation for both of us after two weeks.

With Din awake and our spirits somewhat lifted, we got back on the PCT. It was beyond clear that the trail had only amplified the points of contention in our relationship. The physical and mental exhaustion, coupled with inadequate rest, eroded any buffer that normally kept the peace. With shared gear and personal space, including our quilt and tent, there was nowhere to hide from our problems. We couldn't just ignore the bad things or hope they'd go away. We were within yards of each other 24/7, and if we wanted to make this relationship work, let alone finish the trail, we would have to figure things out.

14

Crater Lake

Crater Lake/Mazama, Oregon
August 16–August 17

B efore starting the trail, we had heard plenty of tales of
"hiker hunger," an insatiable appetite that comes from
walking so many miles and exerting so much effort. Hiker's
bodies simply cannot keep up with the physical demands and,
calorie starved, end up shedding weight. We had tried to mitigate this as best we could in our planning, incorporating whole
foods and minimizing added sugars within our allocation of
two pounds of food per person per day. I wondered if people
lost weight simply due to not having the correct proportion
of macronutrients, specifically enough protein. So we'd made
it our focus to include many high-protein foods, even supple-
menting our daily intake with a scoop of protein powder each.

Not all our food was optimized for perfect nutrition. Starting
in Southern Washington, we were pleasantly surprised to find
all kinds of bonus sweets in our resupply boxes—our friend
Elizabeth had taken to including goodies like peanut butter
M&M's, chocolate bars, Swedish Fish, and Skittles. This was all
much to the delight of Alana, who often proclaims that the fact
that "you can eat ice cream every day" is one of the best things
about being an adult. Months after we finished the trail and
as I was writing this book, Alana said I should write about the
candy. "Why?" I wondered—eating candy is not that special.

A smile spread across her face: Alana had secretly conspired with Elizabeth to include the candy as a "surprise," knowing I wouldn't have added it on my own.

On the trail, our line of thinking regarding nutrition seemed to prove correct. We'd hiked 700-plus miles without experiencing the relentless hunger. Was it really that simple? Was it just a matter of eating sufficient protein and avoiding junk food? The resupply mix-up in Shelter Cove gave us another chance to test our hypothesis. With our scavenged food, we'd be eating more like traditional thru-hikers, munching on less complete and more processed food in the form of energy bars, cookies, and snacks loaded with sugar and preservatives. Sure enough, we found ourselves feeling hungry by the end of the first day, even with a larger quantity of food on hand. If it was just hunger, it wouldn't have been too difficult to deal with. But we also found ourselves sapped of energy and with a newfound cognitive fog. The next town couldn't come soon enough.

I was excited for our next stop at the iconic Crater Lake. The official trail goes around the outer edge of the park, well away from the lake, offering no views of the lake itself. There were a few sections like this, where the path had been routed in a less scenic area due to suitability and regulations regarding horses, as the PCT is open both to hikers and equestrians. After confirming with each other that we were in fact not horses, Alana and I opted to take an alternate trail that went up to the lake and along the rim trail into town.

Up from the flatlands we climbed, hiking through sparse, wide-open forests and grasslands, where I expected to find elk grazing around each bend. It seemed evident that the ecosystem was transitioning to something drier, away from the ferns and leafy, green understory we'd been accustomed to throughout much of the Cascades. As we climbed, we gained a broad view of the surrounding area and where we had traveled. The

9,000-foot high Mount Thielsen rose sharply from the flats in the south, and we reminisced about our break at the creek along its base just a day earlier. As we climbed, the trail began to run parallel to the road into the park, leading both cars and hikers up to the lake's edge.

Unique volcanic spires rose above steep cliffs, which stretched down to the deep-blue water below. We were afforded large views of this unique geographic feature, enough under most circumstances to take one's breath away. But alas, there was something else taken away too—by all the cars and crowds the vehicles had brought to within one hundred feet of the rim. After parking, most people ambled the short distance to the edge for a brief glimpse, content to gaze out and take a few pictures, before heading back to the car and motoring on to the next stop. We looked into one open minivan, where we saw a kid staring at an iPad in the backseat. From outside, his mom asked him, "Do you want to go see the lake, honey?" "No, I'm ok," he said, continuing to tap away.

We continued past the pull-offs and along the rim trail, where just a few hundred yards from the road, we had the trail and views to ourselves. Every half mile or so, the trail would pass another pull-off, full of people just feet from their car, whom we'd quickly pass before returning to relative isolation. What a sad scene this was—a visit to a national park has become a pit stop, somewhere to walk out a few hundred feet, snap some photos, then head back to the car to do the same thing a few more times. I'm reminded of Edward Abbey's quote from *Desert Solitaire*:

> "You can't see anything from a car; you've got to get out of the goddamn contraption and walk, better yet crawl, on hands and knees, over the sandstone and through the thornbrush and cac-

tus. When traces of blood begin to mark your
trail, you'll see something, maybe."

What were these visitors missing from being in their cars?
How did their relationship to the land change when they knew
that, at any moment, they could whisk themselves away, back to
the land of strip malls and concrete? Alana remarked how these
over touristed areas often felt like amusement parks or zoos.
We'd experienced similar crowds and behaviors in other parks,
like in Zion National Park on our Southwest trip the previous
winter. There we ended up stuck in traffic, part of the throng
of motorists driving past dozens of pedestrians and hundreds of
other cars that filled every available spot off the road. That brief
experience was enough for us to change our itinerary and skip
our four planned days of excursions within the park completely.
Crater Lake's rim trail offered moments for contemplation and
appreciation of the lake away from the hubbub. But at times it
seemed that no matter where we looked, we found a disturbed
landscape, like the soft thud of a helicopter traveling overhead
that lifted our gaze from the lake to the sky or the puttering
motorboat on the far side of the lake.

Perhaps it's a fantasy in the modern age to wish for something
different, for somewhere where every last whim and luxury are
not catered to. A place whose treasures require some type of
struggle and discomfort to view and appreciate. A place where
those who wish to see the land can do so only on its own terms,
instead of from within the confines of a car. Ideas like this make
me dream of the National Park Service banishing all private-vehicle travel in the parks. Near the start of the trail, in Stehekin,
Washington, the bus driver had lamented that the park service
no longer lets people drive out to a local waterfall, how now
you had to hike a three-mile trail. Disgruntled, he thought that
since he paid taxes, he should be allowed to see the splendor of

the local environment via the method of his choosing. But that raises the question of whose needs and desires we are catering to. After all, I pay taxes too, and would prefer to keep cars out of "wilderness" and natural areas.

Denali National Park presents an interesting middle ground and one possible solution. For decades, the park has banished private-vehicle travel beyond mile marker 15 on the 100-mile park road. For anyone looking to travel beyond this point, they have the option of biking, walking, or taking one of the many buses operated by the park service. An array of bus schedules and itineraries brings visitors to different spots along the road, from the visitor center near the Parks Highway to Wonder Lake near the tiny town of Kantishna at the end of the road. The predictable behavior of the buses and people staying within their vehicles has led to an environment in which the animals still feel comfortable near the road, which leads to plenty of wildlife sightings and the feeling of a still wild landscape.

During the summer of 2018, while working for state forestry, I had the pleasure of working out of Kantishna and driving work vehicles along the road. Over the course of a few weeks, we made two out-and-back trips along the road, and each time we were eager to see what we would find. Moose lingered in the willows, grizzlies grazed berries off the hillsides, Dall sheep looked down on us from above, and we were even lucky enough to see a wolverine dash across the road. There's no reason that other parks, which have far more infrastructure and generally much higher animal density than Alaska, can't offer the same experience by implementing similar strategies. With traffic jams and crowded trails, it's mindboggling how such a system hasn't already been widely implemented. Zion National Park actually offers something similar, but on a smaller scale, running a shuttle bus for most of the year through one of the most popular segments of the park, Zion Canyon. In its early days, Yellowstone National Park offered a similar service, before giving way to personal car transport. Other national parks, like Arches, Rocky Mountain, and Glacier, have implemented timed entry programs, requiring visitors to obtain a permit and make a reservation to travel through the park at specified times. Some might say Alaska is unique and can support such an approach because of the low population densities, remoteness, and lower visitor numbers, but in fact the parks in the Lower 48, with their very high visitor numbers and resulting impact, show exactly why such a program is essential and should be a widespread practice. Anything else is a disservice to the ecosystem and the American people.

Later in Mazama (Crater Lake Village), we picked up our re-supply boxes, set up our tent in the campground, and went about town chores. We were ecstatic to find Adam there. We'd met him for the first time just outside Trout Lake, Washington, and from there we leapfrogged back and forth until we left the trail after Alana got stung the second time. We had figured by this point that Adam would be far ahead of us, but fortunately for us, logistical issues had kept him holed up in Mazama for a couple days longer than planned. We spent the evening trading stories and catching up in front of the general store, wolfing down cans of chili and leftover pizza, kindly donated by visitors dining at the nearby restaurant.

In the morning, we walked over to the restaurant to grab breakfast with Adam before hitting the trail again. Alana was carrying Din, who was full of smiles after being thrown about in the air. They were walking out well ahead of me until a man stopped them in front of the general store.

"I saw you walking with the pack and the baby yesterday, and thought surely she can't be doing the trail with that baby."

Alana responded, "Well, yes we are hiking the trail."

"Why?"

"For fun."

"Oh, she's not having any fun."

Alana laughed and Din was still all smiles. "She's having fun most of the time."

He scowled and shook his head, saying, "Well, just think of what she'll be doing in the future after having done something like this. She's going to be so tough."

"Uh, yeah, that's kind of the point."

The guy stormed off, and Alana chuckled. The conversation didn't really put us off, but we found it amusing and bizarre. This had been our only negative interaction so far, either on or off the trail.[1] Otherwise, everyone else had been overwhelmingly encouraging and positive. There were multiple younger women who told us that we had opened their minds to what was possible for themselves. Before, they felt that having kids would consign them to a life at home, their dreams of hiking diminished to just that: dreams. They told us that seeing us backpacking with a baby expanded their horizons.

Just a day earlier, we had passed a woman while Din was taking a nap. Alana was out front and let her know we had a sleeping baby. As we were passing, she whispered to us, asking if we were doing the whole PCT. Upon hearing yes, she jumped up and down with a huge smile on her face, raising her arms in the air and silently cheering us on. Luckily for us, interactions like this happened daily, giving us an unexpected morale boost and a greater sense of purpose as we toiled onward.

---

1. It would turn out to be the sole negative interaction over the course of the whole trip.

15

Thunder

Mazama to Hyatt Lake Road, Oregon
Hyatt Lake Road to Mount Shasta, California
August 17–August 23 81 miles

There were times when Din seemed content to ride in the pack for extended periods, with little need of songs or jerky, content to babble away and watch the surroundings pass by. However, there were still plenty of occasions when it was like she'd never been in a pack before and wanted no part of it. One of us would lift her up above the pack, and she'd flail away with her legs, crying, squirming, and evading in any way possible being lowered into her seat. Most times, it'd take just a moment before she calmed down again, going quiet and smiling once she was lifted into the air. Other times, it'd take some walking to do the trick. And, of course, there were the few instances where nothing but jerky calmed her down. Din had always been a very happy baby, usually laughing or smiling wide, but she still had her moments.

Despite our best efforts, sometimes there was just nothing we could do to calm her down and maintain forward progress. Not long after leaving Crater Lake NP, Alana, Din, and I all found ourselves at our wit's end. After a fruitless hour of singing and occasional bribing with rocks and jerky, we stopped in a rare shaded area, amongst live trees in a burn zone. Alana was exhausted and went to lie down fifty yards away, so tired that she didn't even bother taking a sleeping pad, instead choosing to just curl up and bed down in pine-needle duff. Meanwhile, Din, who was supposed to be the one sleeping, bounced on my chest and played with sticks and pinecones. She didn't rest for one second, but was able to play and relax enough to at least ease our frustrations and put smiles back on everyone's faces.

At our first campsite after Mazama, we were surprised when Adam showed up around sunset.

"We thought you were far ahead!" Alana exclaimed.

He was just as surprised to see us: "Hah, I kept waiting for you guys throughout the day, taking long breaks, waiting for you to catch up."

We enjoyed spending more time with Adam, and began traveling more or less together, taking breaks at similar spots during the day and camping close to each other at night. Adam, who was no stranger to babies with two kids at home, wasn't as put off by Din's antics as others might have been (or at least so he claimed). We'd been trying our best to camp alone, away from others, especially as we weaned Din from her night feedings, which often caused her to wail with displeasure. But with Adam, we didn't need to be as conservative with camp spots, and we were thrilled to have the company of another person after spending so much time together as a family.

The days we arrived early in camp were some of the most enjoyable on the trail. Extra time in the evening allowed Alana and I to decompress, taking a break from the racing around and allowing us to relax while Din roamed. On those evenings, we'd take in the views surrounding camp, make a fire,[1] or simply enjoy each other's company. Those evenings became even better when we could share them with friends. Having a familiar face

---

1. In the rare areas and circumstances where it was permitted.

around provided a spark to new conversations and a welcome boost in energy.

Leaving Mazama, we encountered another day of dense smoke, but it eased the next day, replaced by darker cumulus clouds building on the horizon. Those flew across the sky, coming our way quickly and producing loud echoes of approaching thunder. Over the next few days, we'd find ourselves racing darkening clouds that arrived by midafternoon, trying to make progress before they let loose with rain. We took to spending about an hour each day hiding under pine trees, donning our rain jackets and waiting out the storms.

We were thankful for the accompaniment of rain, ever worried about the risk of wildfires. As it turned out, areas farther south wouldn't be as lucky. During one of the late-afternoon storms, lightning erupted in Northern California, in the mountains surrounding Seiad Valley. Instantly, dozens of fires sprouted up, prompting the Pacific Crest Trail Association to close the stretch of the trail from the Oregon-California state line to the town of Etna, California. The closure became the talk of the trail, with southbound hikers debating whether it was worthwhile to find an alternative route around the fires or to skip ahead farther south to Etna or Dunsmuir.

There were even those who had thrown all caution to the wind and tried to push through the fires. Along the trail we met "Shroomer," a well-connected thru-hiker who had been in Seiad Valley the night the fires began. "I watched the fires start on the hillsides. You could see lightning everywhere you looked," he told us. He had arranged a ride out with two extra seats, but the other hikers there wouldn't take him up on it. They started packing up camp at 9 p.m., heading north well after dark into the storm, knowing that there'd be closures and hoping to get on the trail before that happened.

We had found this mentality—the need to hike every single mile of the trail at whatever cost—befuddling, especially when it meant putting oneself and others at significant risk. We figured it had to be people who weren't accustomed to wildfires, those living outside the West, Canada, and Alaska. Without firsthand experience, perhaps they weren't aware of the compounding problems that wildfires present. How help from emergency response is not guaranteed, how the winds can switch in an instant, how you can die from suffocation and smoke inhalation, how fire can travel more quickly than you can walk or run, how new fires can start...and so on. It was remarkable how many hikers seemed to hold the belief that as long as they were on trail, nothing could harm them.

With Din in tow, we weren't inclined to take significant risks or engage in something like 200 miles of road-walking to connect skipped sections of trail. With no point in hiking all the way to the closure at the state line just to be turned around, we debated where to go once we reached Ashland, Oregon, 15 miles north of the state line. This decision was simplified by the fact that my friend Cody lived in Mount Shasta, California, just north of the PCT. Initially, we considered skipping ahead to Etna, but upon realizing that the surrounding air was likely filled with smoke, we planned to reroute farther south to Mount Shasta, and then continue hiking from there.

Two days out from Ashland, we were hiking down the trail, having spent the previous night sharing a cabin with Adam at the Asperkaha County Park Campground. The day before, we had experienced our biggest rainstorm yet, one that forced us to huddle up with half a dozen other hikers under the largest pine tree in the area. Our packs and clothes had been soaked, and we hoped to find some relief and a chance to dry out within the cabin, but without a heat source, nothing really dried. To top matters off, we had forgotten Din's only insulated jacket hanging on a pine tree six miles back, having taken it off once we discovered that it was wet.

The cool air ushered in by clear skies following the storm, coupled with moisture in the air from the wet grasses, made for chilly walking down the trail. Alana was out front, with Din and I in the rear. Crossing a dry streambed, I felt something pricking my calf. I turned my leg out, looking to see what was there, only to find a yellowjacket stinging me. While brushing it off with my other foot, I yelled, "Alana! I'm getting stung. Go! Go! Go!" Without looking back, she took off sprinting for about a hundred yards. I took some antihistamine pills as a precaution and continued, the dull pain in my leg my new companion.

About fifteen minutes later, away from any water sources or streams, Alana got stung. We hurried up the trail once more, trying to put space between ourselves and whatever had stung her. As we ran up the trail, I turned on the inReach and took out an EpiPen. After we felt like we were at a safe distance, Alana took some antihistamines. Unlike the previous incident, we were able to react right away, and she had no allergic reactions like hives. Having already been stung twice that day between us and with only some thirty miles to go before Ashland, we opted to bail out early, and I called Cody. Despite the circumstances, Alana was calm, displaying no symptoms. With no reaction and armed with our medicinal war chest, she felt comfortable trekking on. Cody kindly offered to come pick us up immediately, and within a couple hours we were being whisked away from the Hyatt Lake Road into California. We could only hope that leaving Oregon behind would also leave behind our insect problems.

If our time in Salem was our first *forced* rest of the trail, then our time in Mount Shasta was our first *real* rest. Cody told us that prior to us visiting, he was wondering what we'd want to do. Usually when he and his wife, Caryn, have visitors to their home in town, they take them hiking, biking, and out to do all kinds of other physical outdoor activities. But as an endurance athlete himself, he quickly realized that we'd probably just want to eat food and rest. Right he was about that. We spent a couple days snacking, lounging, sharing meals, reading books, and snacking some more.

One morning I stepped onto the bathroom scale and was confused by the number that stared back at me. Was this thing broken? That couldn't be right. I had started the trail at 175 pounds, without much weight to lose. At Cody and Caryn's, the scale was telling me that in the span of about 6 weeks, I had lost 20 pounds. That was the moment I realized that my lack of energy was not solely a result of inadequate sleep, but also from undernourishment. Alana had lost a handful of pounds as well, but thankfully was in better condition despite hiking the trail AND breastfeeding.

It appeared we had debunked our own theory—that junk food, a lack of protein, and processed carbs were the root problem—regarding hiker hunger. Even when we ate well, our hunger increased and the pounds fell away, causing us to feel like devouring everything in sight. With a more demanding trail awaiting us farther south and our energy levels already wavering, eating would take on ever more importance for us going forward.

HAT CREEK RIM

TRAIL CLOSURES

SEIAD VALLEY

ETNA

MOUNT SHASTA

DUNSMUIR

BURNEY FALLS

OLD STATION

QUINCY

SIERRA CITY

SOUTH LAKE TAHOE

N

BABY CARRIER

LASSEN LAKE SWIM

SAN FRANCISCO

DIXIE FIRE SCAR

NORTHERN CALIFORNIA

16

Northern California

Dunsmuir to Burney Falls State Park, California
Burney Falls State Park to Old Station, California
Old Station to Quincy, California
Quincy to Sierra City, California
Sierra City to South Lake Tahoe, California
August 24–September 16 391 miles

J umping ahead on the trail due to the wildfires gave us an opportunity to see the stark ecological differences between the northern Cascades and the southern end of the range. The chipmunks that we had become accustomed to seeing scurry around the trail were gone; in their stead, we found lizards, darting across the bare ground and under rocks with our passing. Ferns and shrubs gave way to poison oak and an open understory. A thick layer of deciduous leaves littered the forest floor, indicating more diversity in the canopy than the conifers we were used to.

Our animal encounters had increased as well, and we saw black bears, numerous deer, and a rattlesnake. Of the three, the deer would end up causing us the most problems. For whatever reason, perhaps a lack of mineral availability, the deer in the area were salt crazed. They were known throughout the trail community to stalk hikers and their gear at night, looking for morsels of salt. Nothing was safe. They were notorious for coming into camps and nibbling on any gear that was left strewn about, including trekking-poles straps, backpacks, clothes, and even tents. If it had sweat on it, the deer would find it.

I'm not sure how they realized when we would stop, but there were numerous camps where deer would show up within minutes of our arrival. Perhaps the steady procession of hikers stopping in commonly used camp spots was their version of a buffet, and we just happened to show up for feeding time. Early on, we'd head off a dozen yards from the tent to relieve ourselves. There was more than one occasion shortly thereafter when we heard the deer lapping up the urine, just like a dog would with water. As a result, we took to peeing well before we arrived in camp. If we had to go once there, we'd walk a few minutes away, dig a hole, and then bury it. Alana took to pretending she was a deer, both hands raised over her head, and running around camp eyes wide. The sight of her would send Din into bursts of laughter.

Late one day, a mile from our camp spot, we got to experience the deer's aggressiveness firsthand when we came across a buck in the alders, just a few feet off the trail. Instead of running away as we approached, the buck moved forward, jumping through the thicket to get closer to us. We hurried on, to put as much distance between us as possible.

Shouting at the deer from afar and throwing rocks near them to scare them off did nothing to change their demeanor. Presumably after years of the practice, the deer had become emboldened. I took to stacking rocks inside the tent before we went to bed, arming myself for the coming insurgency. After dark, we'd wake to crunching noises on the ground outside the tent. The sounds would come closer and closer, until we would hear an animal breathing and sniffing around the ground. Surely it was a bear, we'd think, accustomed to Alaskan animal behavior. I'd grab my headlamp and peer out from under the tent, only to find a deer staring back at me every single time. They'd freeze in the light, as if they thought that if they didn't move, I wouldn't be able to see them. At close range, a few choice words and rocks would usually send them going. If that didn't work, I'd run out of the tent like a madman, yelling and waving my arms around. We wouldn't usually see them after that.

The terrain changed. Mountains replaced by rolling hills. Old-growth forests replaced by logging areas. We left Dunsmuir heading through an old-growth forest, ascending nearly a dozen miles of long, sweeping switchbacks. By the second day, we'd entered a logging area. Much of the surrounding environment was filled with grasses, stumps, or stands of pines. We passed piles of logs, brush piles, and roots and traversed hillsides overgrown with manzanita. The terrain was dry as a bone, with little water to be found. It was easy to see why Northern California was such a hotbed for wildfire activity. We hoped that the risk of fire wouldn't affect us going forward, keeping our heads down and pushing on.

One of the most significant changes was the absence of crowds. Each day, we'd see only around five people total, going hours at a time without interacting with others. This was a welcome change from our previous sections. In Washington, our average was around sixty per day, and we saw about thirty per day in Oregon. It wasn't hard to see why. The area didn't offer much for the weekend or recreational hiker compared to other locales in the region. There were no sharp peaks, massive mountains, or mystical forests. Without the PCT, the area would undoubtedly be even less frequented, further highlighting its barrenness and remoteness.

Even though we were hiking through areas that we considered aesthetically mediocre at best, the trail still offered plenty of reasons to look up and take in our surroundings. Views of Mount Shasta accompanied us for well over one hundred miles, its snow-capped summit standing high above the surrounding hills. From the ridge tops, we were treated to miles and miles of rolling hills. And with fewer trees, the clear night skies displayed thousands of stars overhead. It was an interesting contrast. Nothing about NorCal strongly stood out among the logging areas and lack of big features. But the animal activity and relative solitude combined to make for an environment that felt alive for the first time on the trail.

Meanwhile, our journey continued to be punctuated by the practical challenges of thru-hiking as a family. One of the core differences between us and the other thru-hikers was diapers. Our daily schedule was largely centered on them, leading us to constantly mull over questions like: Where was the best spot to wash them? When would we need to change her? Did we have enough clean and dry diapers for the day? Outside of the final day before reaching a resupply point, we rotated through a set of six reusable diapers with cloth inserts. Most of them would only serve for about four hours, the two exceptions being the ones with thicker material that we used at night. After that point, there was the risk of the inserts becoming over saturated, leaking onto Din's clothing and the pack, and irritating her skin. So, while other hikers merrily tromped along, stopping where and when they pleased, we were forced to be more strategic. Too many stops and we wouldn't be able to make much progress. As a result, we took breaks with efficiency in mind, stopping to rest and eat snacks near water sources so that we could also filter water and wash diapers.

Ever since Din's birth, we'd largely washed diapers by hand, even at home since we don't have running water or a washing machine. We half joked that washing diapers on trail was even easier than at home since we had access to more water. Alana and I would switch off on washing duty, one of us staying back by the packs to play with, feed, or hang out with Din while the other went about washing. The diapers didn't bother us; we'd largely become desensitized to them after the first week of her life. Part of our diaper system also included bamboo liners, which trapped nearly all the solids. We'd pack these out, resulting in us needing to wash only the pee-filled diapers.

Mindful of not contaminating water sources, we used a series of gallon Ziploc bags to get the diapers clean. We'd fill a clean bag with water, heading well away from the water source to do a wash-and-rinse cycle before wringing the diapers as dry as possible. From there, we'd take safety pins and hang the inserts and diaper covers on the back of our packs. Whenever I was hiking a little ways behind Alana and we passed someone, I'd watch as they stared at the pack and the diapers, swaying to and fro with each step, no doubt utterly confused as to what they were witnessing. A true diaper brigade. On all but the rainy days, everything would dry within twelve hours or less, allowing us to begin the cycle once more.

It had been a little more than two weeks since Alana and I'd started doing the nightly check-ins, and they were already paying large dividends. With everything out on the table, our communication was back to being easy and free, further bolstered by having a formal venue in which to address any grievances. And despite the simplicity of the practice, sharing the things we appreciated about each other had led us to value each other more than before, appreciating the things both big and small we were doing for each other.

We wondered why we hadn't done something like this sooner in our relationship, as there only seemed to be positives. Most nights, neither of us would have anything to address, instead just stating what we were grateful for. However, there were a few nights with more conversation, provoked by feeling taken for granted or not listened to. But instead of being terse, casting blame, and instigating a fight, the statements prompted a discussion, an attempt at understanding, and an opportunity to improve together. With only positive results to show for our early efforts, we opted to keep doing the check-ins indefinitely.

Since we'd skipped the Klamath and Marble mountains due to the fires, the crux of Northern California was hiking through the remnants of the forest burned by the Dixie Fire. California's largest fire on record had left behind a burn area that took multiple days of travel to cross. In such an exposed area with minimal shade, we were nervous that Enedina would be at risk of overheating in the late-summer heat. It was one of the real risks we took in hiking the PCT with an infant. Unlike adults, infants don't have a fully developed thermoregulation system, meaning that they can get hot and stay hot much more easily than adults can, or vice versa with cold. We debated different strategies, whether we should skip ahead or if we could just get by with spraying her shirt occasionally and offering her ample amounts of water. The forecast for the next week made us wary. There were numerous days forecasted to be sunny and in the mid to upper 80s. Could Din handle the heat? Was it worth it?

After resupplying at Burney Falls State Park, we checked the weather again and noticed clouds and storms forecasted a few days ahead, just beyond the heat and right in line with when we'd be traveling through the burn scars. It seemed like the timing could work out perfectly. The trail leading from the park to the outpost of Old Station would be some of the flattest we'd seen yet, so with a couple long days, we could set ourselves up well to take advantage of the conditions through the Dixie burn.

I gushed over the terrain profile, exclaiming how low the elevation changes were to Alana, and fantasizing about trying to travel our farthest distances yet. Most of the time, I was okay with our travel distances, but occasionally I wanted to push beyond and go farther. We'd soon discover that while the terrain was flat, other unforeseen difficulties would make that first day out of Burney Falls one of our hardest yet.

The Hat Creek Fire had passed through the forest just south of Burney Falls in 2009, and fourteen years later, the forest was still undergoing the early stages of succession, meaning that some trees had come up, but they were still young and not yet tall enough to provide much shade. Dark lava rocks made up much of the surface of the trail, storing the heat from the sun and radiating it back up as we passed. To top things off, water sources were scarce, only popping up every ten or so miles. As the day wore on and the sun rose higher, we baked in the 87-degree heat. We shaded Din's legs with diaper inserts pinned to the sides of the pack, sprayed her shirt with water, and made sure we kept enough water for her to drink. There were a couple of times during the day when I turned to check on Alana, finding her face flushed and spent. I would take her hat off, grab my water bottle, and dump its meager, precious contents over her head. Between breastfeeding, chronic dehydration, and the heat, she was struggling to push on. Further compounding matters was her knee, which had swelled up due to the high mileage, despite the flat terrain. Red hawks circled us overhead throughout the day, seemingly in anticipation of us keeling over.

Fortunately, our cooling strategy for Din seemed to be working, as she babbled and bounced about as normal, oblivious to the heat. For much of the day, our throats were parched and our water bottles nearly empty. We yearned to escape the blistering rays of the sun and feel relief from a cool breeze, but shade was in short supply and the air remained calm. Toward the end of the day, we came upon a large tank someone had maintained as a water cache, stopping to fill our bottles and trying to satiate our thirst from its slow trickle. Carrying on into twilight, we ended up hiking 27.6 miles, finishing our longest and quite possibly hardest day yet. From our camp near an overlook, we were rewarded for the day's efforts with a sweeping view of Mount Shasta to the north, backlit by a twilit sky full of pastels. As we settled in, dozens of dragonflies flew around and over our tent. Once the sun dropped below the horizon, we let out a deep breath, finally finding relief from the day in the coolness and dark of night.

Fearing more of the same treacherous heat, we resolved to leave early the next morning. Satellite imagery showed some trees a dozen miles or so ahead, so we tried to leave as early as possible, hoping to put the Hat Creek Rim and its exposed terrain behind us. But there's only so early that you can start hiking with an infant, and we weren't on the trail until after 7 a.m. By 9 a.m., the sun was high overhead, beating down on us. We were still running dehydrated from the day before and were still without a regular supply of water. Needless to say, we were thrilled to come upon some surprise "trail magic" later that morning, a water cache—an assortment of gallon jugs—kindly left under a tree along one of the dirt roads by some local trail angels. Din was asleep, so I continued on with her on my back while Alana stopped to fill the bottles and drink her fill.

Reinvigorated, we hiked the last few miles into Old Station, resupplying then pressing on into a safe haven of ponderosa pines. After more than a week of traveling through logging areas and old burns, our wonder at and appreciation for living trees was near an all-time high. It was a joyous moment for us to walk through the pines, enamored with the neon-yellow lichen that hung from their branches and wrapped around their trunks. We admired how the light accentuated the ponderosas in the late evening, illuminating their trunks and casting long shadows on their far side. Within a few miles, we made camp in the forest, with a gurgling stream lulling us to sleep nearby.

That first day across the flats would turn out to be far worse than anything we encountered later. After we reached the ponderosas, the temperature cooled off and then the clouds arrived as forecasted. Under their protection, we hiked through the burn, finding ourselves worrying more about staying dry and warm than overheating. In the meantime, the aesthetically pleasing contrast between the standing charred trees and the more vibrant understory in the forest ended up making this stretch one of our favorites in the region.

One of the things that plagued us the most throughout our journey was the baby carrier. We had searched far and wide, trying to find something that would be comfortable for Enedina but tough enough for a thru-hike. Quickly, it became apparent that the baby-carrier market was not designed for backpackers, let alone thru-hikers. There were plenty of options, but very few were lightweight and had storage compartments. As I wrote earlier, we'd ended up settling on the Osprey Poco Plus, a carrier with twenty-six liters worth of storage compartments and a sunshade. It seemed the best option by far but would prove to be a hefty load at eight pounds when empty.

We could deal with the weight, but the hip belt was a different story entirely. The pack had an external frame that sat close to the wearer's back, and the lower cross bar went directly across the base of the pack—nothing unusual for an external-frame pack. However, what set the Osprey Poco Plus apart, and what we discovered after only a few days on trail, was that the company had neglected to pad the center of the hip belt, over that lower bar. It was okay for a day, but after double-digit miles, day after day, the bar would dig into our lower backs, especially going uphill. Our lower backs would feel bruised by the end of the day, and we came to dread any time we spent with the pack.

We took to calling the pack the "Horcrux," after the objects in the Harry Potter series where the Dark Lord had placed his soul. In the books, anyone who found and carried the horcruxes would be beset with a foul mood, interacting with others with disgust. The pack did the same for us, stealing a part of our souls with each step and casting a negative light onto nearly every thought. We would snap at each other, lose patience with Din, minimize our own self-care, and do things that didn't make sense, like avoiding taking breaks or drinking water. After long, strenuous days, limited sleep, and worn patience, dealing with this damnably painful pack was the last thing we wanted to do.

From the beginning, we had tried to come up with ways to ameliorate the pain. We stuck all kinds of things—wind jackets, sun hats, small closed-cell-foam pads, pullovers, and more—between our lower backs and the pack, hoping to create some type of buffer. However, most were too thick and would end up creating more pressure, exacerbating the problem. Our luck changed one day in Oregon when we were walking through a lava field and came across a thin, small purple foam pad just lying on the trail. It had a curve to it and appeared that someone had used it to pad their own pack. We picked it up, figuring it was worth a shot. The little purple pad worked perfectly, offering just the right amount of padding between our backs and the bar, preventing us from even noticing the frame most of the time. The resulting dramatic decrease in pain also led to a dramatic improvement in our moods.

The pad served us for hundreds of miles, until we lost it when hitchhiking into Old Station. We'd been picked up by a woman named Cary and her daughter, out for an open-ended adventure after fleeing the smoke around their home in Ashland, Oregon. Tossing our packs and ourselves into their van, we neglected to see that the pad had slipped onto the shoulder unnoticed, leaving us back at square one with the carrier. But Cary and her daughter were incredibly kind, not only taking us where we needed to go, but offering us fresh fruit from their neighbor's trees, different kinds of snacks, and well wishes. We came to treasure such occurrences along the trail—people who gave to us weary thru-hikers with no strings attached, in hopes of helping us along.

Before the start of our trip, my friend Rich had mentioned that we'd be amazed at the number of people who went out of their way to help us simply because we were attempting something difficult. At home, we had an assortment of friends willing to watch our dog, lend gear, give advice, and ship resupply boxes. Then, during our journey, there were our friends Tyler and Cody, who picked us up and dropped us off at the trail at a moment's notice, then housed us and fed us for multiple days; Delia in Carson, Washington, who passed up hiking with her grandkids to take us into town; Karen in Carson, who gave us groceries; Leslie and Lynn, who picked us up in Sisters and Quincy respectively, taking us where we needed to go; and many others who offered rides. There was also plenty of trail-centered help, like from the notorious trail angel "Devilfish", who maintained multiple hundred-plus-gallon caches of water and refused to take donations. Or others who maintained smaller caches with snacks along the way. We were blown away by the generosity and the idea that people wanted to help, often spending not only their time, but their own money, to do so.

It was hard for us to say how much of this kindness was due to us having a baby versus just being run-of-the-mill PCT thru-hikers. There were many people who told us how having a baby would help us, making it easy to get rides and seek assistance. The reality was often the opposite, especially in Northern California. There, many drivers were apprehensive of transporting us without a car seat, even despite our assurances. We found some irony in this—that in the supposedly libertarian, rugged-individualist "State of Jefferson," the people were most worried about complying with the law.

Help or no help, Din was becoming more and more of a celebrity on the trail. After months of travel, word of our attempt had traveled up and down the PCT. We increasingly came across people who had heard of us from others elsewhere. Everyone was incredibly kind, asking about our adventure and wishing us well. At least once a day, we were stopped and asked to take our photo. People continued to be inspired by what we were doing, and we increasingly used that as motivation to trod on.

Near the halfway point of our journey, at Sierra City, California, we took a break to head off-trail for a few days and join friends for a reunion of sorts in the Mojave Desert. On the way down, we soaked in hot springs, filled ourselves with food, and enjoyed great company. The rest of our break would lead to more of the same—time spent with friends, chatting and hanging out around a bonfire under a night sky with countless stars.

Despite taking a few days off from the trail, we found that we still weren't recovering nor did we feel fully rested. On-trail or off-trail, our problems were mainly the result of not getting adequate sleep. Off-trail, we'd engage in less physical activity, but that was often counteracted by worse sleep for Din, presumably from being in a new environment. As a result, even when we took "breaks," we would return to the PCT feeling even more tired. Sleep became our one focus and the determining factor for how each day would go, but unfortunately it was also the factor over which we had the least control. My journal during the trip reflects that, with most of the entries talking about hoping for sleep or lamenting poor sleep from the night before:

August 29: "...Practiced walking with Din between us back and forth before bed. Quite a few other people nearby on the creek. Away from the creek we have company, too. Some deer walking around making noise behind our camp. Hopefully they let us sleep."

Aug 31: "Dragging my feet all morning. Dead tired and my shoulder was bothering me. I think I slept in 30-min stretches. Din was up frequently, and then there was another deer crashing around camp..."

September 6: "...Din struggling to go to sleep, screaming and crying, so I took her to the lake outlet to stare at the water, which calmed her down. Still a struggle but down at last."

September 7: "Cry, cry, and cry some more. Din was nearly inconsolable throughout the night and into the morning..."

September 15: "Din woke up at 10 p.m. last night just screaming on top of my chest. Alana took her and tried feeding her, but she wouldn't take it. A few minutes of confusion, and then she settled down after we took her jacket off. It was the theme for the night and the rest of the day. Upset and bothered about something, but we can't figure out what. Maybe a wonder week?..."

We'd get immensely frustrated at night as a result, just wishing for some continuous rest. But the trip and confined quarters accentuated Din's poor sleep, and after two months on-trail, we'd only had one night during which we slept more than three hours in a row. Yet come morning or midday, Din would win us over once more, playing with us, babbling away in her pack, and exclaiming, "Yee, yee, YUH!" over and over again. We were dead tired yet couldn't help but smile.

Fortunately, time on the trail generally got easier. Din became more comfortable in the pack later in the day, and there were even a few days when we found ourselves racing sunset with her still mostly content. However, there were still difficult days and moments when she was fussing and we still had to continue, either out of desire to set ourselves up or there not being any water and/or campsites nearby. In these situations, I would resort to carrying Din in my arms instead of trying to calm her down in the pack. She would stop crying and fussing immediately, and become very excited. We would walk down the trail mimicking each other's noises, waving at random things as I tried to make her laugh. These were possibly my favorite moments on-trail, and sometimes I wished we could have hiked the whole PCT this way. The farthest I had managed was 5.5 miles. I wondered half-seriously whether my arms would be strong enough for a whole day's worth of carrying by the time we reached the desert.

It wasn't until we were well past the halfway point that we learned how truly different our hike was compared to everyone else's. One night we were camping with our friend Vista, who emerged from her tent around 9 p.m. to tell us about the George Foreman documentary she'd just watched. *What?! People were watching movies*? Turns out, it was far more common than we thought. In town, people would download movies and TV shows, watching them sporadically throughout each section. *What a life!* While they watched sitcoms and movies, our nightly entertainment was me singing a rendition of "Mary Had a Little Lamb" fifty-three times to get Din to sleep while Alana dealt with diapers and other chores, before we did our nightly check-in, and maybe—if our heavy eyelids hadn't slammed shut—wrote in our journals. During the day, while others listened to audiobooks, music, and podcasts as they hiked, our "audiobook" was recounting Dr. Seuss stories from memory, and our songs were our own renditions of lullabies and folk songs like "I've Been Working on the Railroad." Over and over and over again.

Atop Dick's Pass, high in the Desolation Wilderness with a view of more than a dozen alpine lakes, we chatted with a couple from the United Kingdom on a multi-week trip around California. They were amazed by our thru-hike, having wondered if they could do the same thing themselves (sans baby) in the future. The woman remarked at one point, "You guys will probably have massive culture shock after your trip." But neither of us were so sure. On the PCT, we'd crossed numerous roads every day, passed through towns every few days, and often walked through commercial developments like logging areas and ski slopes. On top of all that, there were the people. We'd continue down deeper into Desolation Wilderness from Dick's Pass, finding a landscape that was far from desolate. Here, we were reminded of the crowds in Washington's Goat Rocks Wilderness, as once again we passed well over one hundred people out and along the trail, reminding us of just what was missing from the experience.

We weren't certain that many other thru-hikers would experience culture shock either. We were surprised to hear so much talk of town while out on the trail. Some fellow thru-hikers would scheme about how they could quickly get to town to party, which led to long days and them hiking many miles beyond the norm. The constant physical wear and tear didn't combine well with the effects of alcohol. To mitigate the damages, there was widespread use of ibuprofen, as well as amphetamines, according to some rumors. For a large subset of hikers, it seemed as if town was the attraction rather than the time spent in the forests and mountains, a place to consume stimulants and indulge in other excesses.

Our interests couldn't have lay further in the opposite direction. After all, the primary reason we'd chosen to go south in the first place was to avoid that party culture, prizing roadless stretches and a deeper experience in nature, where animals outnumbered people, over hotels and stays in town. John Muir seemed to have thought something similar, writing in one of his journals:

> "Tell me what you will of the benefactions of city civilization, of the sweet security of the streets—all as part of the natural upgrowth of man towards the high destiny we hear so much of. I know that our bodies were made to thrive only in pure air, and the scenes in which pure air is found. If the death exhalations that brood the broad towns in which we so fondly compact ourselves were made visible, we should flee as from a plague. All are more or less sick; there is not a perfectly sane man in San Francisco."

As we got closer to the Sierras, the carrier continued to wear on Alana. By the time we had reached South Lake Tahoe, the constant rubbing had caused not only bruising, but what seemed like more significant damage. A lump had formed on her lower back, putting her in nearly constant pain. We swapped packs, and I took to carrying Din most of the time. To further ease Alana's burden, I began carrying more weight than normal. With the addition of a few days' worth of food, I heaved the load up to my shoulders and bumbled on down the trail, some fifty pounds of gear, baby, and food on my back. The going had just gotten harder for both of us.

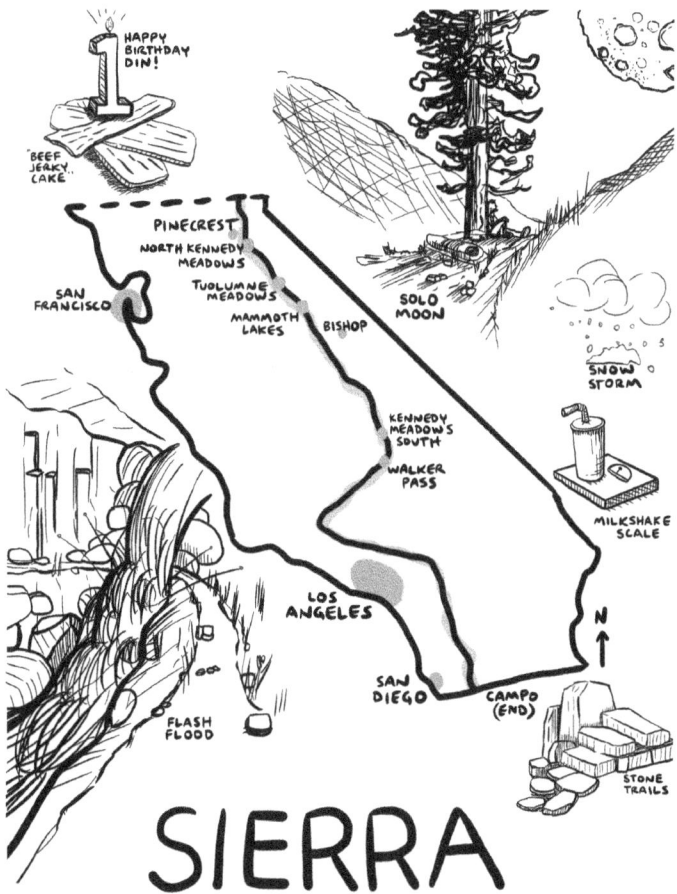

HAPPY BIRTHDAY DIN!

"BEEF JERKY" CAKE

PINECREST

NORTH KENNEDY MEADOWS

SAN FRANCISCO

TUOLUMNE MEADOWS

MAMMOTH LAKES

BISHOP

SOLO MOON

SNOW STORM

KENNEDY MEADOWS SOUTH

WALKER PASS

MILKSHAKE SCALE

LOS ANGELES

N

SAN DIEGO

CAMPO (END)

FLASH FLOOD

STONE TRAILS

SIERRA

17

The Sierras

South Lake Tahoe to Pinecrest, California
Pinecrest to Tuolumne Meadows, California
Mammoth Lakes to Bishop, California
September 17–September 30 235 miles

Sometime in the first few days of September, Din and I were walking the aisles of the Grocery Outlet in Quincy, California, when a woman, recognizing us as thru-hikers, stopped us to ask about our trip. She was skeptical about us heading into the mountains at that time of year and asked why we were going so late.

"We're actually ahead of schedule and positioned to get through the mountains well before the first average snowfall." I said.

She dismissed this and talked about the hurricane two weeks earlier and other recent storms that had dropped snow in the mountains. She then paused for a moment, glancing from me to Din, and with a stern face said, "I'd be looking for snow."

As if traveling with a baby wasn't enough, moving into the Sierras upped the ante for us. Along with increasingly steeper terrain, the weather had started to change. Gone were the days full of sunshine, replaced by afternoons with dark, rolling clouds, roaring thunder, and lightning. Knowing there would be a forced break sometime in the afternoon due to the weather, we hiked as far we could in the morning before finding shelter under pine boughs come storm time. At night, we took to snuggling closer together in our quilt for warmth, the temperature dropping lower than what we had been accustomed to. Autumn was upon us.

We braced ourselves for our first encounter with the lingering snowpack, unsure how much we'd find up high and how we'd fare ascending and descending the north-facing passes. With the help of the fire closures, we arrived in the mountains far earlier than planned, setting us up well to avoid the onslaught of new winter snow. But snowstorms remained a possibility at any point, one that would drive us from the trail, and so we maintained a sense of urgency. It seemed like we had been hurrying all of our journey to get to this point, only to find ourselves racing ahead yet again.

At Carson Pass on Highway 88, there was an information station with a scale, giving us another opportunity to weigh our packs and ourselves. After learning that I'd lost twenty pounds, I was curious to check the results of my efforts at stuffing my face full of food every opportunity I got. I had become a milkshake connoisseur, sampling each town's offerings. Bert's Café in South Lake Tahoe impressed with its generous servings, giving me not only the glass of peanut-butter banana milkshake I'd ordered but also the extra in the mixer. Then there was the near-miss with the blackberry milkshake in Old Station; arriving at Hat Creek Resort to a closed kitchen midday, we were thrilled to learn they could still whip up milkshakes. However, not all of them met our expectations, like the disappointing pre-made, packaged chocolate peanut-butter cup shake at Red Moose Cafe in Sierra City. But by far and away the best shake was in the least likely of locations—Burney Falls State Park's visitor center, where I had a huckleberry milkshake I *still* think about.

When I stepped onto the scale, the number hovered around 150 pounds, possibly dropping into the 140s. My bulking strategy had not shown any results. Not only had I not gained weight, but I'd lost an additional five pounds. I found myself at my lightest in a decade and was puzzled trying to figure out why. Initially, I had thought that I had lost upper-body mass, but still being able to carry Din around in my arms for 5.5 miles made me skeptical of that. Looking down at my legs, I found my answer. My previously muscled quads and hamstrings had been reduced to toothpicks. Our calves seemed like the sole muscles left on our legs, with everything else whittled away. We were literally hiking our butts off.

The following afternoon after one of our breaks, clouds rolled in again and it started to rain, unrelentingly. We stopped for a moment to don our raincoats. But to our surprise, the rain quickly turned to hail. It fell lightly at first, but increased in intensity until it was thundering down. The balls got slowly bigger until they were about marble sized. We ran along the open trail, trying to reach a protected spot, ultimately taking cover under a small stand of pines. The wind blew strong, sending the hail down at an angle and into our faces, forcing us to the leeward side of the trees. We watched as the spherical pellets coated the forest and trail, the grasses, dirt, path, and plants buried under a layer of white. Din looked on in awe, undisturbed by the action and speechless in the carrier sheltered by the wide trunk of a tree. The nearby creek quickly doubled in size. Was it worth setting up our tent? We were on a steep slope without any ideal spots, so we decided just to wait it out. After maybe half an hour the storm lightened up, and we emerged from cover and continued down the trail.

We soon realized that the rising waters in the nearby creek were a snapshot of what had happened to all the waterways. Creeks that were running clear just an hour before were now rushing torrents of murky water. A mile later we came to Noble Creek, which ran muddy and strong and appeared impassable at its intersection with the trail. The creek roared across the trail, dropping off a dozen feet just to our left and rushing farther down the drainage. With Din in tow, the added risk of crossing there didn't seem worth it, and we decided to seek other options. We scouted around, looking downstream below the drop and finding a spot that would've probably worked. However, with the slopes bare of vegetation and covered in hail, there was no safe way down to the water without a high risk of falling. We wandered upstream, finding a big rock in the middle of the channel that brought us within two feet of the other bank—though the landing rock on the opposite side was coated in hail. It didn't look like we could cross without getting wet, so we decided to just ford, finding a shallow spot just upstream of the rock and wading across.

Once on the other side, our adventure continued. The route back toward the trail went above a set of small cliffs on the edge of the creek and along a steep slope. Neither of us felt any confidence in navigating that safely, so we were on to plan B: laboring straight up the 45-degree slope in front of us, looking to intercept the trail up top. We reached a stand of trees about halfway up and found it difficult to go much farther. It was there that I realized we'd gotten ourselves into a far riskier situation than desired, with no obvious way out. Descending back to the creek wasn't feasible due to the steepness and the hail, plus it would leave us exposed on a slick slope.

The clouds had lightened and the hail had started to melt, turning the hillside into a muddy, slippery mess. We had trouble finding footing. No more than ten yards above us were solid rocks that would lead us up to the top and off the hillside, but they were blocked by a yard or two of open slope without adequate footing. Din had started to cry, upset with all the erratic movement from scrambling up the hillside. I tried to calm her as my mind worked in a million directions and my stomach churned.

"I don't like this, baby." I said to Alana, who was standing farther downslope.

"Can you get over there?" she asked, pointing to a tree with a solid base just yards away.

"It's too exposed—there doesn't seem to be anything to hold onto."

Eventually, with a couple of large steps and the assistance of some pine-sapling roots, we were able to haul ourselves up to the rocks. From there, it was no more than a thirty-second scramble to the top. I let out a huge sigh of relief, then watched as Alana negotiated her way to the top. We'd lucked out after some poor decision-making. The moment we'd decided we were going to get our feet wet, we should've just returned to the regular crossing at the trail.

Up above, the trail was wet and still covered in icy pellets, but offered quick passage once more. We crested a pass, crossing through a wire fence up top. Sunlight beamed down on the valley and mountains beyond. There was no sign of hail on the other side, and the way the light fell on the mountains made it feel like we'd stumbled upon Eden, a welcome sensation after getting beaten up by the storm.

High winds met us the next day as we hiked toward the 9,600-foot Sonora Pass, north of Yosemite, and descended to the highway. Fed up with the inclement conditions and high altitude, Din fussed and fussed, inconsolable in her perch atop the pack. I ended up carrying her in my arms once more, taking her down the hillside toward the road.

There we were surprised to see Cookies, a trail angel who, along with his partner, Sailor, hosted hikers at their home in Pinecrest. We had arranged a stay with him via satellite messaging earlier, but there had been no mention of a ride, and we were expecting to have to hitchhike the thirty or so miles to their home. Along with two other hikers, Mango and Pierre, we piled into Cookies's Prius, descending 4,000 feet from the pass and into town.

We had originally intended to only spend the night, but a winter weather advisory and forecasts of snow, high winds, and temperatures around freezing at high elevations kept us around Pinecrest the next day. We ambled around town, walking near the lake and discussing our journey into the mountains. Alana was nervous, wondering about the cold and whether we had enough clothes to keep ourselves and Din warm. The nights had already become much colder, leaving us chilled and searching for extra warmth within our sleeping quilt. As the season wore on and we reached higher elevations in the Sierras, the temperatures were bound to keep dropping.

Anticipating this, we had shipped our cold-weather gear to the resort Kennedy Meadows North, picking it up the following day along with another bear can.[1] The management units[2] required carrying a bear can for much of the Sierras, so we were left with no choice but to oblige, needing two to fit all our food. My friend Cody had lent us one of his, which we had carried without issue since Sierra City. One bear can was no problem. I

---

1. Each with a height of roughly 13 inches and a diameter of almost 9 inches.

2. National Park Service and National Forest Service.

was able to strap it on the top of our gear pack without noticing any additional burden. But two bear cans? With the addition of our winter jackets and long underwear, along with six days' worth of food, our gear pack was overloaded. We were maxing out the attachment straps with one bear can, and there seemed to be no feasible way to fit two. We looked at the Horcrux—er, baby carrier—to see what we could do. There was nowhere near enough room to store a bear can inside the limited storage spaces, and the outside of the pack lacked attachment points. After a bit of thinking, Alana was able to finagle a rigging system out of paracord, lashing the canister to the back side of the baby carrier. If we weren't a unique sight before, we surely were now.

I heaved the pack over my shoulders, and we ambled up to 11,000 feet, the highest point yet of our trip. If the pack had weighed fifty pounds a week earlier, I figured surely it was now closer to sixty. The south side of Sonora Pass marked our entrance to the big mountains, hiking above tree line, and our first significant patches of snow on the trail. While Alana hiked along unfazed by the terrain, the combination of dehydration and high altitude had given me a headache, and I worried that the same was true for Din. Atop the ridge, she cried and cried, despite feedings, snacks, and breaks. We couldn't figure out what was going on—whether it was the altitude or something else. The lack of clarity spurred us on, and we descended rapidly back into the forest and made camp as the last bit of alpenglow lit up the mountains.

The following day, a stretch of flatter trail led us past the clear waters of the semi-alpine Dorothy Lake and through grassy meadows into Yosemite National Park. Alana had taken to carrying Din again due to the large amount of food and gear in the gear pack, but the Horcrux continued to frustrate her, aggravating the bump on her back. It had gotten worse, swelling to the point that she couldn't lie down or sleep on her back without pain. I told her we should switch, and took a few days' worth of food out of the gear pack, replacing them with diapers to help reduce her load. But she didn't mention things improving after a couple breaks so I ended up taking the diapers back, stuffing them in the bear can, and re-shouldering the baby carrier. A heavy pack! I was thankful for the gentle terrain.

Later in the day on a break near the cascading waters of Falls Creek, Alana mentioned that the town of Mammoth Lakes—900 miles from the PCT's southern terminus—might be the last stop for her. The news caught me off guard. I was frustrated that she appeared to have already made a decision that, at the time, seemed to come out of the blue. Looking back, it was obvious that the heavy packs, increasingly difficult conditions, and pain were accruing. As we continued along the trail, her decision became all I could think about. What would we do? Was there any way to make our travel easier and make Alana more willing to stay?

We crossed Falls Creek toward the end of the day, and as we were putting our shoes back on, on the other side, we started talking about it again. The conversation grew heated, with emotions rising and frustrations with the trail and each other spilling out. Alana said that she'd "wished for each day to be over every morning since starting the trail again in Sierra City," nearly two weeks earlier. I ended up feeling annoyed with her, for not hearing about any of this during our nightly check-ins and also for her deciding to quit instead of trying other options after we'd made it as far as we had: over 1,300 miles.

We had promised each other that if either of us felt fed up with the trail, we would quit, change plans, or do something else, together. But faced with this reality, I became selfish and was more concerned with my own interests—namely, finishing what we'd started—than the desires of my (injured) wife and the three of us as a family. Alana said that I could continue by myself through the Sierras, and, if she felt better, maybe she'd meet me for the final stretch.[3] But after having done so much of the trail together, I was uncertain if I wanted to continue alone. We were left at an impasse but in the meantime resolved to get off at Tuolumne Meadows, in the Yosemite high country.

We had heard from others earlier on the trail that twenty miles per day elsewhere is more like fifteen miles per day in the Sierras. We weren't sure what to make of this. Was this just due to most people experiencing big mountains for the first time on the trail, or were conditions actually that much more difficult? We'd been through the Cascades in Washington—surely the Sierras couldn't be much worse. After we hiked a couple of days farther into Yosemite, it became apparent that the terrain indeed was different. The trail brought us up one canyon, down another, and up another again. Again and again and again. Gone were the dirt paths with a light duff layer of pine needles. In their stead were cobblestone paths and deep sets of rock steps. Our legs strained under the heavy loads of our packs. Coupled with the dwindling light, we found ourselves working all day, striving to hit our twenty-mile daily goal. We only managed that once, otherwise replaced by the new normal of walking full days of sixteen to eighteen miles, with six thousand feet of elevation gain and the equivalent in loss.

Amidst the climbing, the trail became busy again, and we found ourselves leapfrogging with a large group of other thru-hikers. We'd bounce back and forth with them on the

---

3. She'd backpacked through the Sierras before, and said she felt okay missing this section.

trail each day, camping nearby at night. One evening, we hiked past sunset into the darkness until we reached the Glen Aulin backcountry campground near Tuolumne Falls. After putting Din to sleep, Alana and I ate together on the step of a shed, watching as the other hikers set up their tents and then gathered for a group dinner by headlamp, sharing stories and laughing in a large circle. Days like this left us pondering what could've been if we weren't carrying a baby, and part of us wished that we could join their fun. Still, we agreed we wouldn't change what we were doing, even if we could. Trail life with Din was no better or worse—it was just different.

The approach to Tuolumne Meadows the next morning introduced us to some of the finest scenery on the trail so far. Water rushed down creeks over granite ledges and falls. The morning air was cold, accentuated by the plumes of steam emanating from the Tuolumne River's surface. The river ran through a valley covered with grassy meadows, with granite mountains and rounded domes rising along the edges.

Our arrival in Tuolumne Meadows coincided with perhaps the most noteworthy event of the trail up to that point: Din's first birthday. Despite the natural splendor that surrounded us, she couldn't have been less pleased. Hiking out to the road from Glen Aulin campground, she fussed and wailed, inconsolable despite our best efforts. I got frustrated that we weren't making good enough time, since we had arranged to meet one of Alana's friends for a ride out and didn't want to keep her waiting. After making no progress, we cast our plans aside once more and returned to the present moment, taking a break and feeding Din before continuing. Content again, she relaxed, falling fast asleep within the pack, sleeping until the parking lot, where we ended up being early for the meetup anyway.

Perhaps ironically, Din often became most excited when we saw roads and passed through towns. She would hoot at the sight of passing cars, bouncing and shaking feverishly with excitement from her perch in the Horcrux. Towns offered the opportunity for a higher density of people, and just like on the trail, she would greet everyone we passed. We'd be walking through the grocery store and someone would be looking at products on the opposite side of the aisle, prompting Din to let loose a "HI!" Sometimes, people would pretend not to hear her and go about their business, but more often than not, people would happily engage and she would become all smiles while repeating, "Hi! Hi! Hi!"

We went about our usual chores in Mammoth Lakes, splurging on a room at the Motel 6[4] and stopping at the grocery store to stock up on ice cream and snacks, as well as food for my next section. Most of the afternoon we spent lounging on the bed, video chatting with Din's grandparents, who wanted to share in the birthday festivities. Having signal once more brought in a slew of messages, including one from my friend Tyler, who lived near Walker Pass, farther south on the trail.

"By the way you're getting within easy driving distance from me. If you need any support at all, hit me up." He messaged. To which I responded, "Hah. Funny timing."

I explained our situation to him and our tentative plan for me to carry on into the Sierras solo. He was willing to host Alana and Din until I made it farther south, even offering to pick them up immediately. For her part, Alana was more than okay skipping ahead and recuperating in the desert with Din. We decided we could reunite there, continuing south into the Mojave if her back healed and we all felt well enough.

With Alana and Din taken care of, I set about trying to figure out my own plans. I was torn between wanting to be with my family and spending more time in the mountains. I

---

4. Fortunately, we didn't have to spend the $500/room the motel charges during winter peak ski season!

began gathering information, looking at what I might face if I pressed on. We had originally planned for our next resupply to be at Independence, after 110 miles of hiking. But with a lighter pack and the ability to move faster, everything changed. I figured I could hike longer each day, making it all the way to Kennedy Meadows South, a small community with assorted services, without resupplying, 204 miles away. I pored over the maps, looking at the passes and obstacles that lay before me, envisioning taking them on by myself.

Meanwhile, Alana had been messaging friends on the trail, updating them as to where we were and seeing how their walks were going. Suddenly, she gasped.

"Guess who's in town?!"

"I don't know. Who?"

"Adam! And he's leaving tomorrow."

We hadn't seen Adam since we'd parted ways in Oregon. He had continued south on the PCT, going on his own adventure on dirt roads and unintentionally trespassing through ranch-lands when trying to hike around the wildfire trail closures. He was behind us for a while, but had hurt his knee and skipped ahead, after recovering, to catch up with other friends. Another series of events had kept him in Mammoth for a few days, and we arranged to meet him at a local bakery. We caught up, trading stories of our experiences in Northern California, before talking about the section ahead. After explaining our situation, I proposed that he and I link up, and we agreed to continue south together.

Going with another person relieved some of my anxiety —the anxiety of being trapped in my own head and focusing on things beyond the trail. I thought back to many of my solo trips in Alaska and beyond, where I had wrestled with the fear of being by myself and feeling small in the state's vast expanses. There was the initial trip to the Brooks Range, nine years earlier, during which I'd left early after feeling intimidated by the big landscape. Then later that summer I'd been in the Lower 48 on the Colorado Trail, where a nocturnal encounter with a big black bear had driven me off the trail. And the many times since then, when I had found myself yearning to be out in the mountains, but once there alone, found myself worrying about grizzlies and other predators, despite years of experience. All those feelings and thoughts evaporated with the company of another person. As such, none of them surfaced the next morning, when I knew I'd be heading on with Adam. After seeing Alana and Din off on the bus to Inyokern, where they'd meet Tyler, we caught a ride to the Horseshoe Lake Trailhead, continuing south into the mountains.

I'd spent over 1,300 miles hiking with Alana and Din, and heading out without them was strange. I had lost the aura and mystique that we carried on the trail due to hiking with a baby. By myself, I was just another thru-hiker. With that, there was no longer the need to recite Dr. Seuss stories or sing my usual array of lullabies. At breaks, I just sat down and ate what I wanted and looked around. There were no diapers to be changed or washed. And at night, I didn't even need to set up the tent; instead, I simply laid my sleeping pad beneath a piñon pine and slept under the stars and the moon.

One reason I'd felt apprehensive about continuing solo was the weather forecast. As usual, most of the forecast comprised of sunny days and cooler nights. However, some days on, they were calling for snow and daytime temperatures closer to freezing. Alana tried to reassure me prior to leaving, telling me that it would be fine, knowing I had the tools and experience to deal with any situation. And with Adam, I felt more confident that we'd be able to deal with whatever came our way, though worries about snow remained in the back of my mind.

On Thursday, our second morning out, that thought quickly came to the forefront. We ran into a friend of Adam's, who asked if he had heard about the snowstorm forecasted for the weekend. In a rare spot with cell reception, we stopped and discussed as we pulled up forecasts and charts from the National Weather Service. What we read didn't provide any reassurance. A winter storm warning ran Friday night through the weekend, with eight to twelve inches of snow at higher elevations for Saturday alone. Adam was a little skeptical, unsure of the forecast's accuracy, while I didn't want to leave anything to chance.

Neither of us had any interest in turning around and heading the 30 or so miles back to Mammoth. But pushing on didn't seem like it would offer us many bailout options if the weather took a turn. Independence was nearly 90 miles ahead—more than 3 days of travel—and if the storm came in, we'd still be hiking there during its height. Looking at the maps, we noticed Bishop Pass, a 10-mile-long side trail that led from the PCT to a trailhead at South Lake, 22 miles by road from the town of Bishop. That became our plan, and we set off right away, needing to navigate some 60 miles of trail and multiple 12,000-foot passes in less than 36 hours if we wanted to beat the storm.

Our days started in the dark hiking by headlamp and ended well past sunset with the headlamps back on. We forded rivers in the dark and walked below granite mountains and along alpine lakes by day. The alpine reminded me a lot of Alaska, with lingering snowfields that resembled glaciers, and willows, low-growing vegetation, and lichens spread around the lakes. Adam and I talked frequently of Alaska, sharing stories of his visits to the state and my experiences living there, as well as our shared fascination with the Alaskan legend Dick Proenneke, a renowned naturalist. The conversation and the scenery transported my thoughts farther north, occasionally causing me to wonder why I had traveled so far to do something so similar.

I continued to think about Alana and Din, hoping that the break from the trail was mentally restorative for Alana and wondering if the bump on her back was healing. Thoughts about continuing to the PCT's southern terminus came and went. Traveling through the desert would be interesting, but in all honesty I'd lost the stubborn fire that had caused us to butt heads over a week earlier. I was torn between spending more time in wild environments versus spending time with my wife and daughter. Seeing the heart of the Sierras, I found myself content with what we had done. If, after reuniting in the desert, Alana or both of us decided that the day heading into Tuolumne was our last on the trail together, that would be okay with me.

The Sierras marked a return to the crowds, and with many of the people we passed, the conversation turned to the coming storm. We traded information, seeing if there were any updates and how other people were planning on dealing with it. Some presented conflicting information and doubted the forecast, while others were looking for the quickest way out to town.

Adam was still uncertain of the forecast, and we continued to talk it over. The risks associated with snowstorms in the mountains are very similar to those posed by wildfires, in that the problems can compound rapidly. Snow-covered rocks and trails create poor footing and make for slow passage, while the increased chance of being wet and cold leads to a greater risk of hypothermia. A new snowpack of possibly more than a foot, followed by freezing to near-freezing daytime temperatures, would mean slow travel for days, potentially stretching our food rations thin. The ensuing snowmelt following the storm would raise rivers and creeks, making crossings more hazardous. And finally, the clouds and inclement weather could prevent emergency personnel from arriving not for hours, but days. The margin for error was thin, and the rewards for taking chances seemed very small.

While we rested near 12,000 feet in the High Sierra at Muir Pass, an updated weather report from the National Weather Service on my inReach sealed our decision. The message gave

12-hour forecasts for 72 hours beginning Friday evening, with each period mentioning heavy snow and low temperatures. Clouds rolled in as we were descending Muir Pass. As we ascended Bishop Pass, we watched as they darkened, increasing in volume and breadth to cover the mountains. That last day brought us up and over two 12,000-foot passes over 32 miles of trail. We topped Bishop Pass just after sunset, descending and walking along the lakes below in the dark. By the light of our headlamps, we made it to the trailhead just before 9 p.m., setting ourselves down next to a dumpster sheltered from the increasingly gusty winds.

We were out of the woods regarding risk but not yet out of the elements, and still needed to figure out how we'd get through the night. The parking lot was full, but we didn't find anyone heading back to town at that hour, forcing us to make camp. Steep slopes and rocky terrain surrounded the lot, meaning there were no flat campsites to pitch a tent out of the wind. The sole protected, flat spot we found was a small patch of gravel on the leeward side of the pit toilets. Without any alternative, we plopped down there, nestling in our sleeping bags and wrapping ourselves in our tents like burritos, trying to fall asleep. Rain fell not long thereafter, eventually turning to snow. We woke to people coming and going from the bathrooms, as well as the arrival of emergency personnel, out at 1 a.m. on a search and rescue mission for an oxygen-depleted hiker. The snow covered our tents, and I awoke later to a wet sleeping bag. Cold and unable to sleep, I retreated to a dry spot inside the restrooms on the concrete floor. It was not the most pleasant night, and I was thankful my family had been spared the experience.

Come first light, I waved down the first car leaving the parking lot and explained our situation, and we hitched with them into sunny Bishop. Adam and I wandered over to a local bakery, happy to be dry and warm once more. We refueled while watching the dark clouds envelop the high peaks to the west, below which we'd walked just hours earlier. With the storm set to last the weekend and to be followed by days of near-freezing temperatures, Tyler offered to pick me up, with Alana and Din in tow. Adam stayed behind in Bishop to mull over his next steps, while we fled south to Tyler's home in the high desert, where the storm brought only a smattering of rain.

Adam and I would later learn how those who'd decided to continue along the PCT had fared. The conditions had ended up being mild that Saturday, with only two to four inches of snow on the ground at the passes and plenty of sun breaks. But Sunday had turned for the worse. About eight inches of snow fell, and high winds blew it around all afternoon, limiting visibility. Hikers had problems finding the trail amongst the snow, while also dealing with slippery ground, wet fingers that couldn't use touchscreens, and headlamps that ran out of batteries in the cold. Others decided to forgo travel, hunkering down in their tents and weathering out the storm. The conditions made for quite a few adventures, and at least this time, ones we were happy to miss.

18

Into the Desert

Walker Pass, California
October 1–October 7 14 miles

A t Tyler's, in the high desert near the southern end of
the Sierras, we regrouped to figure out our next steps.
If we were going to continue, we'd need to fix the baby-carrier
situation. Continuing with it farther south didn't seem like a
sustainable option, nor one that either of us were looking forward to. We asked a friend to send out our Ergo, a lightweight,
sling-style baby carrier. Our thought was that if we could combine that with a fanny pack, we could potentially ditch the
Horcrux. It would be ultralight backpacking, family-style! We
headed out into the surrounding desert from Tyler's to test the
Ergo, hiking faint paths and old Jeep trails up mountainsides
and through washes. Days into our stay, my legs still felt heavy,
weary from the constant travel and inadequate rest. Short hikes
up nearby mountainsides or even on flat ground would leave me
wanting to rest.

The Ergo worked fine for carrying Din on these shorter outings, but it didn't seem like she'd be content in it for a long
day on the trail. Her position so close to whoever was carrying
her also dramatically increased the risk of overheating for both
parties. Not satisfied with this alternative, we decided that the
Horcrux really was the best option.

Alana's back continued to improve; the lump continued to diminish and caused her no further pain, which allowed her even to sleep on her back again. A week and half's worth of rest had done wonders for her legs and spirit. I had no interest in hiking the rest of the Sierras alone, without my family, so we talked about continuing south from Tyler's into the desert. We looked at the map, figuring that the 600 or so miles to the Mexican border would take us another four weeks. With the end nearly in sight and the mountains behind us, we agreed to carry on, figuring that we could finally travel at a more relaxed pace. After resupplying once more in town, we bid farewell to Tyler atop Walker Pass, thanking him profusely at the trailhead and hopping back in the saddle.

The trail shot up steeply from the road, passing through thickets of rabbit brush that buzzed with dozens of bees. Toward the top, after climbing a couple thousand feet up and traveling seven miles, I found myself plodding along sullenly. It was hot, a few dozen gnats swarmed around our heads, my shoulder hurt, my knees ached, my legs felt heavy, and Din was fussing. On the ridge, we came to a small clearing and dropped our packs, taking a rest near some small boulders. Alana played with Din as I took in the surroundings, looking out over the desert flats to the east and at the towering Sierras lining the horizon to the north. The break had done nothing to ease my discomfort, and I said to Alana, "I'm not sure I want to do this anymore."

"Really? Then let's be done with this and just go back to Tyler's."

I looked down at the sand, picking up a small stick and breaking it into smaller pieces as I thought things over. Was this it? What about going all the way to Mexico? What about all those who had cheered us on? Would we be letting them down? The questions swirled in my head, but the stressors and realities of our circumstances kept me grounded. After a few moments, I softly said, "Okay."

We loaded up our packs and headed back down the trail we had just climbed, finding a clear spot to camp for the night about half a mile later. After heading south for around 1,500 miles, making constant forward progress, it felt strange to backtrack. The appeal of ending at one of the terminuses is that they offer a marked ending point, but I imagine the feeling is still the same. After months of hiking and living outdoors, it was strange to know that the next day, this would all be over. Just like that, our circumstances would change—no more wondering where we would sleep, if we had enough water, and if we were making good time. We put those thoughts to the side as we dug into our food supply, still ravenous despite our extended rest the previous week, eating our fair share of our multiday snack supply before settling into our tent for the last night of our journey.

I went back and forth on my decision throughout the night, not getting much sleep. Despite its imperfections, I'd grown to love life on the trail and the time we spent outdoors as a family. Did I really want to be done? Or was this just a moment of weakness? Was I content with what we had accomplished? Was I okay with foregoing the rest of the desert and leaving the PCT behind?

By morning, with rested legs and a clearer head, I had flip-flopped, convincing myself that I wanted to push on.

"Ugh, you always do this!" Alana sighed, adding that hearing me say that I wanted to be done was one of her happiest moments on the trail.

"We just have a few weeks left, then we'd be done with everything," I pleaded. But Alana had no interest. It was possible that I could persuade her, but at this point what would be the cost? We had agreed early on that if one of us felt like it was a death march, we would stop, and it was beyond evident that we had pushed past that point. Our time on the Pacific Crest Trail was over.

Descending the final few miles to the road, I mentally rewound through many of the events and memories from our almost three months on the trail. I began to think of the things that would be different off-trail and what we wouldn't be experiencing anymore: the simplicity that comes with having all you need on your back; spending nearly every moment as a family outdoors; the satisfaction that came from reaching our daily goal via our own physical efforts; and the memories of Din gaining confidence in herself and her movements, interacting with the natural world.

We'd traveled nearly 1,500 miles on foot as a family. Many had doubted us prior to the trip and said that hiking the whole thing was not possible. We ended up feeling that's not true, but also that it wasn't really that important. Our goal from the start was to spend time as a family outside and do something that was immersive, fun, and challenging. Having largely achieved that, we were leaving the trail with memories for a lifetime.

The discussion that morning had started us off on the wrong foot, and coupled with another disagreement about logistics, had led to Alana hiking well out in front. With nostalgic thoughts in my mind and a sadness about leaving the trail, I tried to savor the moment, plodding along at a slower pace than usual. By midday, when our ending point, the campground near the road, came into view, I whistled ahead to Alana, motioning for her to stop. Din was asleep in the pack, so I hurried to catch up. Once I reached Alana, I grabbed her hand with watery eyes, continuing to feel a sense of appreciation for what we had done and what we would be leaving.

Reluctantly—still frustrated over my change of heart that morning—she held my hand, and we walked side by side for the final few hundred yards. We got to the trailhead, and I implored, "Can't you appreciate what we've done? All the time we spent outside as a family? Together?" But my questions had the opposite effect, prompting an argument.

"No—why do we always have to do things your way?" Alana said. "Then you make me hold your hand while we end the trail! I didn't want to do that."

I motioned for us to go sit in the shade off the trail. Alana talked about value differences, frustrations with life experiences, and not feeling listened to. I listened as best I could, pushing back on her points that arguments and frequent discussions like these made us incompatible. We sat for an hour in the shade, her airing her grievances, me trying my best to listen. Without a happy ending but in need of water, we pulled our packs back on and headed toward the highway for our final few miles of travel.

Cars and motorcycles flew by us as we hiked along the shoulder of the highway. A couple miles in, Alana started cracking jokes. I motioned to some large pinecones along the road, and we stopped to look at them, comparing them to others we'd seen near Hat Creek Rim, what felt like a lifetime ago.

"I don't want to fight you, baby."

"I know. I don't either."

"I'm sorry."

"Me too."

Din babbled away at the trucks and motorcycles. A mile more took us to Tyler's driveway, and what officially marked the last steps of our journey. Halfway up the driveway to his house, with a few hundred yards to go, Alana sidled up closer to me.

"Hey, come here. Give me your hand," she said taking mine in hers.

"What?"

Giving me a wide smile and nuzzling close, she said, "This is when it matters."

Lizards scurried by our feet, desert buckwheat blew in the wind, and the sun shone brightly down on the Joshua trees and mountains beyond. We walked over the sand, hand in hand, with smiles on our faces and Din babbling away on my back. Everything was going to be okay.

Epilogue

T hroughout our journey, we often wondered what kind of lasting effect, if any, the trip would have on Din. Four months post-trip, it's clear that the trail had a notable impact. No matter where we are, she wants to be outside, hanging by the door and saying, "This, this," asking us to go out and explore. Once outdoors, she runs around with abandon, her laughter and shouts filling the air as she looks around. We'll never know the full extent of how the trip shaped her, but we have no doubt about its positive role in her growth.

About a month after we left the PCT, Din started walking, quickly mastering the skill and wanting to walk everywhere. Months earlier, Alana and I had romanticized the idea of Din taking her first steps on the trail. In hindsight, it's clear that had that happened, it would've quickly derailed our trip. While it would have eased the burden on our backs, our pace would have slowed to a crawl, with Din stopping every few feet to check out something on the ground. Nonetheless, at 16 months old, she is well on her way to taking after her parents, walking up to three-quarters of a mile at a time on her own.

In many ways, the trail was different than we had expected. Knowing what we know now, we would not have attempted what we did given the circumstances. It was extremely optimistic to believe that Din's poor sleep habits would improve on the trail. Coupled with our aggressive pace, we'd cooked up a recipe for physical and mental exhaustion. With some slight modifications to our overall goal and pace —like slightly reducing our daily mileage, allowing ourselves more time, and not trying to hike the whole trail— this could have been largely mitigated and would have significantly increased the quality of our experience.

Despite the challenges, we're grateful for the experience and strongly believe that it has been the best thing we've done for Din so far. We went into the trip thinking that it was *our* adventure and that Din was along for the ride. But early on, we realized how wrong that was, how we were doing *her* trip and we were just the facilitators—a fitting metaphor for parenting in general, if there ever was one. We watched as she grew, learned to see, explore, and take joy in her surroundings. She rolled with the punches, through long, hot, dry stretches and cold, blustery, rainy days.

Furthermore, the trip also served as a pressure cooker, intensifying existing challenges within my marriage with Alana. The relentless stress, fatigue, and unpredictability tested our resilience and adaptability, pushing our relationship to the brink. Yet, it was this very pressure that forced us to acknowledge our issues and develop better communication skills, ultimately strengthening our bond and laying a more solid foundation for our future together.

I share our story hoping to inspire others, whether you're contemplating a significant challenge, adjusting to the dynamics of life with a newborn, or seeking to spend more time outdoors with your family. Let our journey stand as proof of the extraordinary discoveries that await when we embark on ambitious adventures with our loved ones. I encourage you to dream big, value moments with those dear to you, and immerse yourself in the wonders of our world.

Until next time, Happy Trails.

Appendix A: FAQ

How far did you go each day?

Initially, we planned on 17.5 miles a day in Washington, 20 miles per day in Oregon, and 19 miles per day in California. We ended up doing 20 miles per day in Washington, 22 miles per day in Oregon, and about 20 miles per day in California. Our longest day as a family was 27.6 miles, near Hat Creek Rim in Northern California.

What was your biggest challenge?

To our surprise, Din's naps—by far. She could fall asleep no problem in the pack, unless there was novel stimulation, like people walking by. The sound of others' greetings would wake her instantly, leading us to hike anxiously when she was asleep, craning our heads around each bend, in fear of seeing someone coming our way. If she didn't sleep during the day, she'd sleep poorly at night, meaning we would sleep poorly (or not at all) as well. By the end of Washington, we had devised a strategy that solved most of our issues: whoever wasn't carrying Din would head out in front, verbally warning oncoming hikers and making hand signs that Din was asleep and to please be quiet.

How much did your packs weigh? Did you switch off?

The contents of our packs were dynamic. Daily, we switched what was inside and who was carrying what, including packs and Din. Our base weight was around 21 to 24 pounds for our gear pack, depending on what part of the trail we were on, and roughly 31 pounds for the baby carrier. On top of that was our food and water weight, which also varied greatly. We carried more water in sections where there were long, dry stretches, and hardly any when water was flowing abundantly. For an average section, we carried about 4.5 days of food (at 2 pounds/day/person), with the lowest total being 2 days and the maximum 6.5. So all that being said, our weights varied greatly and were never really consistent. In the Sierras, the pack with Din was often between 50 and 55 pounds, whereas at other times it was only around 30. The gear pack also varied, from its maximum of around 45 pounds to around 25 pounds, like on the last few miles into a resupply stop.

What did Enedina eat? What did you eat?

She was still nursing on the trail, so the bulk of Din's calories were breast milk. However, she also ate anything that we ate. We brought a variety of snacks, including but not limited to: jerky, Cajun nut mix, "raw cookie dough" nut mix, chocolate, peanut butter, dried mangoes, dates, and chips. For dinners, we ate: rice and beans, cheesy mashed potatoes with bacon, lentils and rice, pesto noodles, and peanut noodles. Until the last two weeks or so, we did not tire of our food and found that it gave us the satiety and energy we needed.

Did you have extra gear for your daughter?

No, not really. We brought diapers and clothes for her, which included a rain suit, but no other personal gear. We did bring a couple of pacifiers, but one fell off the pack early on, and then by Oregon she was over them anyways. Otherwise, no bottles (she drank water out of a regular plastic bottle with a sport top), toys from home, or backpacking-specific gear. See Appendix D for more detail.

What do you do for work (i.e., are you rich)?

No, we are not rich. We did not win the lottery, are not trust-fund kids, and do not earn six figures. In short, we live simply in a small home, source much of our food ourselves, and place value on spending time together. Fortunately, it turns out that this doesn't cost much, allowing us to have expenses that are a fraction of the average person's in the Western world. Living intentionally allows us to save up money and take extended periods off from work, like for this trip.

Isn't life dangerous on the trail? Did you feel safe?

There are bears, mountain lions, and maybe even bigfoot along the trail. But generally, we felt far safer on the PCT than in towns along the way. On the trail, nobody that we met, including ourselves, carried weapons like a gun or even bear spray (many women do carry pepper spray). Far from roads, we knew that the only people we'd find on-trail were the other hikers. In small towns and along forest-service roads, there was always the potential for someone driving around up to no good. The trail community is close, and the use of the FarOut social mapping app helps alert people to any potential dangers (human or otherwise). Anecdotally, we don't know anyone who experienced any issues, including solo female hikers.

Do you have Instagram?

Yes! @jackmcclure24. After the trail was over, I posted a day-by-day account of our trip. You can find that and much more there.

I also have a blog, animaltreks.com, where I posted a few trip summaries along the way. I have written many other posts about trips in Alaska and various aspects of our life there as well.

If you'd like to contact me with questions, typo corrections, feedback, and/or angry tirades, email me at illcarrythebaby@gmail.com.

Appendix B: Adventuring with Little Ones. Strategies & Tactics

The following should be taken for informational purposes only, with the assumption that your child does not have any kind of special health condition. For those with special health conditions, talk with your doctor first. The following advice should not be seen as specific to thru-hiking, but is also applicable to shorter, multiday backpacking, cycling, rafting, or other outdoors-based trips with children.

Adults with Kids can Do Everything Childless Adults Can Do

There were multiple instances on our trip when we passed someone and, after seeing Din, they remarked about how they had young kids as well. We would always ask, "Where are they?" The response was often something along the lines of, "Seeing you, we should've brought them. I don't know why we didn't."

Unfortunately, there seems to be a belief in modern Western society that children don't belong in the outdoors, where an unending array of dangers await, like wildlife, poisonous plants, rocks, water sources, mud, sharp things, and strangers, to name a few. To protect their young, parents elect to shelter their children, keeping them inside and "out of harm's way." But with this approach, they in fact end up doing the exact opposite.

While children are smaller and at an earlier developmental stage than adults, they are neither incapable nor inherently more fragile. Humans have evolved to withstand a variety of stressors, environmental ones included.

Making it Fun

The easiest way to make the experience positive for everyone is to make it fun. *Duh,* you say. *That's obvious.* But when the inevitable happens, like your kid missed their afternoon nap, is now crying inconsolably, and you're tired from hiking with a forty-five-pound pack for a dozen-plus miles with more to go, it becomes hard to detach and keep the end goal in mind. The best way to go about this will vary from family to family. Some families will prefer spending a lot of time in camp or on breaks along the way, while others will be interested in hiking longer distances and spending more time on the trail. It's best to find out what works well for everyone in the family and do something along those lines. Forcing any member of the family to go against their interest for prolonged periods is unsustainable and bound to create negativity around outdoor family trips.

A kid's world is smaller and believed to be filled with far more wonder than that of their parents. As such, even the smallest of things can become a source of enjoyment, like splashing in a trickling stream, looking at rocks, watching insects move, and playing with sticks and logs around camp, to name a few. If you use your imagination and the environment around you, you can create a rich environment in which everything becomes an opportunity for interactive fun.

The Power of Distraction

Despite all the potential for fun, kids can get tired, cranky, and bored (just like adults!). At these times, parents can employ one of the most magical tools of parenting: distraction. There were moments on the trail when Din would get bored from just sitting in the pack and wanted to do something else. For whatever reason at those times, a break wasn't in the cards, so we'd distract her with things like singing songs, telling stories, making animal sounds, and talking about the forest around us. On other occasions, we'd take pieces of bark, pinecones, sticks, or grass, passing them back to her and let her examine them. She'd become engaged once more, and we'd continue happily plodding down the trail. For older kids, this experience can be more interactive, whether as some type of game or simply a conversation.

Not Operating by Your Own Schedule

There are times when none of the distractions work and you're at your wit's end. Maybe there are just a couple miles to go before that waterfall/camp/viewpoint, but your kid is screaming their head off. These scenarios showed us that we weren't always the ones in charge, and that our schedule would have to go by the wayside. As noted earlier, each stop was often dictated by the needs of our daughter, whether that was due to being hungry or needing a diaper change, a nap, or simply entertainment and a change of activities.

Making sure everyone gets adequate rest goes hand in hand with the above, and better ensures you can accomplish your own goals. This is applicable not only to the kids, but to the parents as well. Any member of the family who remains tired from the day's activities will not only be unable to recover physically, but mentally as well. Pushed too far, that same parent can become a liability, with the other parent having to bear the brunt of childcare and trail chores.

Fatigue can color our moods and, coupled with the ever-present challenges of spending extensive time outdoors, can lead to a negative experience. Just like a "stitch in time saves nine," resting early on when you're tired prevents burnout farther down the trail. Take naps, make recovery a priority, and change plans if need be. I'm not saying that you shouldn't push yourself physically; only that you should avoid redlining for long periods, which can lead to injury, burnout, and the end of your trip.

Food, Food, Food

Like many adults, kids don't function well nor enjoy the experience when they are hungry. It's therefore important to carry enough food, in terms of both variety and quantity, to keep them satiated. If you're bringing new meals on the trip, it's worth having everyone try them in advance, to save yourself an unpleasant surprise later.

While food serves as an essential source of energy, it can also be used as motivation for kids when they are bored or not excited about going farther. One family who hiked 1,000-plus miles on the PCT with three kids under age 5 used peanut butter M&Ms to get their kids to hike up to 15 miles a day, incentivizing them along the way. We'd do the same with Din in the pack, passing back jerky, dried mangoes, and huckleberries.

Adverse Conditions and Emergency Scenarios

When times get tough, it's essential to have a contingency plan for yourself *and* your younger companions. The responsibility of taking care of others doesn't permit you to perform at anything but your highest levels, no matter how tired, soaked, or exasperated you are. Each person will know the limits of their abilities and should adjust accordingly. It's worth asking yourself how you will handle a medical emergency not only for your kid, but for your spouse/partner. If your spouse becomes injured or ill, how will you handle both your patient and your kid(s)? In adverse conditions, like cold or rain, can you ensure that your kid stays warm and dry, even if it comes at your expense? It's worth running through various scenarios in your head, examining all the possibilities, so that you are prepared and ready to act if they occur.

I highly recommend taking as many wilderness-medicine courses as possible, too. The gold standard is a wilderness first responder course, but a wilderness first aid course is a good introduction if you can't do the former. Alana and I have each taken over half a dozen medical classes, and have found the skills and knowledge gained from them to be invaluable. The hope is that you never have to put your abilities to work, but if you do, it's better to act from a place of knowledge and experience rather than flying by the seat of your pants.

In our experience, one limitation of these courses is that while some delve into how to apply the material to children (it's often the same or very similar), they do not illustrate the difficulties of managing an adult patient while also taking care of a child. If you take one of these courses and are interested in going out with your kids, I would ask your instructor for scenarios that involve both medical and parenting issues (like a hungry kid, dirty diaper, or a kid who's cold or wants to be with mom, etc.).

Medical Concerns

But what of medical risks? you ask. There currently is no peer-reviewed literature that has anything negative to say about kids spending time outdoors. The reality is the opposite, with an overwhelming number of studies discussing the positive effects that time outside has on childhood development and well-being, and the negative repercussions resulting from kids spending more and more time indoors.[1] Spending time in nature improves their motor and neural development as well as their sense of well-being. If your doctor tells you that it is not appropriate or safe (and your child has no medical condition), I would ask them to show you some supporting literature and I'd seek a second opinion.

That said, there are a couple of things to keep in mind. Younger children, mainly infants and young toddlers, do not have the same ability to thermoregulate as we adults do. That means that when they get hot, they have a harder time cooling down, and vice versa. This is something to be cognizant of

---

1. As an example: Summers JK, Vivian DN, Summers JT. The Role of Interaction with Nature in Childhood Development: An Under-Appreciated Ecosystem Service. Psychol Behav Sci. 2019 Nov 5;8(6):142-150.

when traveling through areas with extreme temperatures, lack of shade, high winds, or other inclement weather.

Another thing that has increasingly become a concern in recent years is wildfire smoke. Outside of very young infants (<6 months), the recommendations for children are the same as for adults. Above an AQI (air quality index) of 150, it is recommended that you limit time outside. Above an AQI of 200, outdoor time is considered hazardous, and the EPA recommends avoiding prolonged activity outdoors. If you'll be traveling in fire-prone areas or areas with the possibility of wildfire smoke, it's worth establishing backup plans and figuring out possible bailout points in advance.

Appendix C: Economic Thru-Hiking and Adventuring

There's a common perception that doing something like the PCT requires spending a small fortune. Somehow, walking in the woods and sleeping on the ground have been transformed into an experience reserved for the elite. This hasn't always been the case for outdoor ventures, with people traveling throughout the woods with little to no money for centuries. Hell, for most of human history, people lived in and off the woods completely without money. As a result of this modern perception, we had some people give us searching glances when we told them our plans and even some who asked if we were trust-fund kids. The reality is that, with just a little bit of planning, hiking the PCT (or embarking on your own long-duration adventure elsewhere) is well within reach financially.

There are a few numbers floating around for the average amount that a PCT hiker spends each year. REI has an article[1] that details a broad range of costs, with the average hiker spending from $4,000 to $10,000. On halfwayanywhere.com, the author conducted a survey of 2022 PCT thru-hikers.[2] With 953 respondents, the median spending value was $9,593. Almost $10,000! This number boggles my mind.

Our total spending for the trip ended up being just over $6,000. Total. For 2 adults and 1 baby. Or roughly ~$3,000 per adult total or $1,000 per adult per month. In other words, we had managed as a family to spend just over half that of the median hiker on the trail. While we didn't finish the PCT, our total expenditure wouldn't have changed much if we had, and our monthly costs would have dropped, as we had bought and prepared food and supplies for the entire trail in advance. Finishing the trail would've meant a few more dollars out of our pockets for shipping our remaining boxes, snacks in town, and maybe a night in a hotel, but likely would not have exceeded an additional $500. We had 5 nights in hotels, 1 night in a hostel, and ate at 8 restaurants. The bulk of our expenses were related to food on the trail. We ended up spending about $19/day on food, with about one-third of that being the cost for shipping boxes to ourselves. Shipping boxes was one-sixth of our total cost; food expenses (including restaurants) were just over half of our total cost.

The easiest way to minimize costs on a thru-hike, bike trip, or backpacking trip is to avoid hotels and restaurants. At a minimum of $100-plus a night and $15–20 per person per meal, respectively, spending a lot of time in town is the fast track to

---

1. Source: https://www.rei.com/blog/hike/how-much-do
   es-it-cost-to-hike-the-pacific-crest-trail

2. Source: https://www.halfwayanywhere.com/trails/pacifi
   c-crest-trail/pct-hiker-survey-2022/

blowing through your budget. Knowing this, we made a point of avoiding hotels unless we were injured or absolutely had no other option. In most stops, there are often free or low-cost opportunities to pitch a tent, with plenty of amenities like laundry, showers, and places to charge electronics. We would take advantage of those and gorge on food from the grocery store. For less than half the cost of a meal in a restaurant, we could get twice the volume of food, returning to the trail full and with an extra spring in our step (well, sometimes).

Beyond hotels and food, the next major line item is gear, and it's here where hikers' fascination with the latest and greatest materials drives up costs. Surely you cannot do something like hike the PCT unless you have a brand-new Cuben Fiber backpack, a 1,000-fill down sleeping bag, and trendy synthetic-based clothing that will keep you cool and warm and make you hike faster. While this high-tech gear will greatly assist you if you are trying to set speed records, for most people it's far from necessary. Whatever will keep you comfortable in cold, hot, wet, and dry conditions for months will work. You don't *need* to buy new gear if you already have something that's most of the way there. For example, does it really make sense to spend $500 to get a tent that's 1.5 pounds less than the one you already own?

We approached the trail with the mindset that we'd use what we had and borrow or source the rest from friends whenever possible. As avid outdoorspeople, we already had almost everything on hand. Over the course of our preparations and trip, we only ended up buying five things: an MSR pot to cook our meals (new, $35); an Ursack bear bag (new, $90); an HMG Southwest 70 L pack (off eBay, barely used for $270); a bug liner for our tent (new, $100); and a water filter (bought new while on the trail for $60, after borrowing one that didn't work from a friend and having ours lost in the mail). $555 in total. With more planning, most of those costs could have been eliminated or severely reduced.

First time out hiking? eBay, thrift stores, garage sales, Craigslist, and gear swaps are your best bet for finding good gear at lower prices. You could put together a good kit from these options, likely spending well under $1,000. Tell your friends about your trip. In our experience, most people are eager to lend out gear if they have extra or are not using it. If you borrow something, remember the principle of returning it in a better state than you found it.

Making your own gear is another option. With a sewing machine and a little fabric, you can make your own tarp, quilt, and more. There are plenty of video tutorials on YouTube. With no prior experience, Alana borrowed a sewing machine from one of our friends and made our 35-degree double quilt for the trip with just ~$70 of material and a few evenings of effort, sewing something that would have cost us upwards of $350 bought readymade elsewhere.

Each person will have to determine their priorities and align their spending accordingly. Do you really like restaurants and want to eat in all the top spots along the way? Great! Just realize that you're going to need a bigger budget that you'll have to save for. It's easiest to make financial decisions in your regular life if you already have a target number in mind for your trip. For us, our average spending per adult per day on the trail was $33. To use our numbers as an example, each time you spend $33, you can see it as one day's worth of spending on the trail, and then budget accordingly. If you're living alone, consider sharing a place with a roommate or two. In urban areas, you could save $1,000/month or more, or $12,000 over the course of a year. That alone would be enough to fund a year's worth of time on the trail at our expense level. Already living with someone? You'll have to look elsewhere for saving opportunities, always asking yourself: *Is what I'm spending money on worth foregoing X number of days on the trail?*

There is no shortage of inspiring stories of people who have done adventures on little to no money. The adventurer Alastair Humphreys biked around the world for four years, spending a total of $8,000. Laurie Lee, author of *As I Walked Out One Midsummer Morning*, had no money when he walked through Spain, and earned his daily expenditures by busking. John Muir famously hiked throughout the Sierras with just a tin cup and a loaf of bread. Others have biked across the country with food as their only expense, staying in tents or on couches via WarmShowers hosts along the way, spending hardly any money. As these examples indicate, it's not the doing of the thing itself that's expensive, but the things that go with the doing. Money is certainly one factor in each trip, but it should not be the limiting one.

Appendix D: Thoughts on Gear

As I wrote earlier, ultralight travel can make trekking a far more enjoyable experience. A lighter pack, in which you carry the bare minimum, lets you travel farther, faster, and without the mental or physical burden of unnecessary weight. Under certain perspectives, this style and mindset could be seen as a sacrifice. But doing without does not have to mean suffering. Like with other aspects of life, a substitution of skills for gear or expensive luxuries can lead to high-quality experiences. For example, if I am skilled at picking out campsites with soft duff, I can travel with a lighter (thinner) sleeping pad and still have a great night's sleep. And if I'm experienced in wilderness medical training, I can use things I'm already carrying in case of an emergency, instead of carrying specialized single-use gear. Along those lines, multipurpose gear can work wonders to help reduce your load. In our case, Alana brought a pair of thick, fuzzy socks which she would wear on the coldest nights. During cold days, the socks served as extra pants or gloves for Din.

Many people use "going ultralight" as a reason to get the latest and greatest gear. While lighter gear is nice and can certainly facilitate a better experience (especially if you're carrying a baby), it's easy to go too far. The professional adventurer Andrew Skurka coined a term for this, dubbing it "stupid light"—it's the same idea as "Penny wise, pound foolish," with people skimping on gear without giving any thought to the repercussions. On the trail, we were often asked what our favorite piece of gear was. This question stumped us, as there wasn't any one piece that was irreplaceable. Alana and I are gearheads only to the extent that we find something that works. If it doesn't work, we'll try something else and adapt.

In that vein, ultralight is not the end-all, be-all. If you're not able to get your pack down to X weight, that's okay. On more than a few occasions, people complained to us about certain pieces of gear, and we'd make a suggestion that would increase their pack weight by six ounces. Unironically, they would respond with, "Every ounce counts!" (Oh right, as if we hadn't thought of that when we decided to carry a twenty-pound baby around!) Unless you're trying to set speed records, after a certain point, a handful of ounces really doesn't matter that much.

The most important gear is the stuff that gets you out there. Besides, there are often other ways to get a higher return. If, say, you have an extra twenty pounds of your own body weight to lose, doing so will help your performance far more than cutting two pounds off your gear. If you don't have anything to lose, consider how you can increase your muscle mass to make carrying a heavier load less burdensome. Due to our fitness, our average distance was close to the average hiker's, despite our carrying packs that usually weighed double or triple what theirs did.

Something that I undervalued is being protected from the elements at night in the tent. We started out with a mid-style tent, without a floor or a bug liner. While the mosquitoes weren't as bad as back home in Alaska, it only takes a few to disrupt a good night's sleep. Ants would also frequently crawl into our tent, and while they mostly didn't bite, we'd awake to them crawling on our legs and feet. We ended up getting a bug liner two weeks into our trip, and it made a massive difference in sleep quality. Mice can also be an issue in highly-trafficked areas, and a sealed tent (usually) keeps them from scurrying over your head and/or your gear during your nightly rest.

Specialized items for babies or kids aren't necessary. If you head out into the forest, your kid doesn't need many, if any, toys or personal gear beyond his/her clothes and diapers. A small toy might be nice, but in our experience, it is tired of quickly and is ignored for things like rocks, sand, pinecones, and other local attractions. This is another opportunity to use the skill of making-do, using the forest and local materials as entertainment, carrying less while still having loads of fun.

On Backpacks for Carrying Kids

For those looking to head out with infants or toddlers, a child carrier will be one of the most important pieces of equipment you'll bring. Unfortunately, at the time of this writing (January 2024), there are very few options that work well for multiday backpacking. Maybe this will change going forward, but currently, nearly every child carrier on the market is catered to day hiking.

As I wrote, we used the Osprey Poco Plus pack, which had the most amount of storage of any child carrier we found, at twenty-six liters. It also has a sunshade, which was an important feature to keep our daughter out of the sun on hot days and dry during rain showers.[1] The downsides are that it's heavy, weighing eight pounds empty, and there is no padding in the center of the hip belt, leading to bruising of the wearer's lower back, as Alana experienced. The only other real alternative is the Deuter Kid Comfort Pro, which also has a sunshade and

---

1. It's water resistant, not waterproof, but it never leaked.

weighs slightly less at seven pounds, but only has fourteen liters of storage. No other pack of this style has more than twelve liters of storage, making them nonstarters for multiday-trip purposes.

For those couples who can fit nearly all their gear into one pack, I would suggest pairing up a fanny pack with an Ergo carrier for child carrier. The fanny pack holds toiletries, electronics, and miscellaneous small gear, while the Ergo carrier lets you carry your infant/toddler in either the front or the back. It is the lightest-weight setup by far, with the possibility for the carrier and fanny pack to weigh in under 2.5 lbs. The closeness you get to your child with the Ergo carrier is both an advantage and disadvantage: your child can be right next to you and feel comforted, but this proximity also subjects them (and you) to a greater chance of overheating. Some Ergo models have a breathable mesh to help with this issue, but you're trading off protection from the elements like you'd get using a backpack with a sunshade.

The last option we considered was a newer carrier called the Trail Magik. The product is basically a pouch that attaches to the front loaders of a normal backpacking pack. The company claims that the design allows the weight to be transferred from the front to the back, allowing one to get the benefits of storage from a regular pack while also comfortably carrying their kid. We found out about this toward the end of our time on-trail, so we didn't end up checking it out. It seems worth exploring, assuming that the carrier does actually transfer the load to your back; my only concerns would be a lack of ventilation and weather protection, as with the Ergo carrier.

Some people have asked me about wearing a regular backpack and then carrying their child in front. I have also heard of others doing the opposite: using a child carrier on their back and wearing a regular backpack on their front. I would not recommend these setups for longer durations. Humans have not really evolved to carry much weight on our fronts, and the load from these arrangements will likely cause lower-back strain, tougher travel, and lower mileage. Better to trim the fat and figure out how to make do with only one pack per adult.

Diapers

One of the trickiest things to figure out was diapers, but we ended up with a system that worked really well. Disposable diapers are the easiest to use while traveling, but you need to pack them out, and once soiled, they become bulky and heavy. Our solution was a hybrid system of disposables close to town (within about a day's travel) and reusable cloth diapers everywhere else. For each section, we settled on bringing six cloth diapers, each consisting of an outer cover and two cloth inserts, along with five disposables. For the cloth diapers, we also added a bamboo liner sheet that we bought online. This captured the bulk of the solids, making the cloth inserts less of a disaster and far easier to clean along the trail. We'd pack out the liners and wipes,[2] throwing them out in each town. The number of liners and wipes differed due to the varying distances of each section. I'd recommend figuring out how many times your child needs their diaper changed each day and basing your estimates off that. We assumed two liners per diaper and an average of two wipes per changing. We added in a couple of extra liners and wipes to each total to account for any irregularities.

The washing process was simple. We'd take one of the gallon Ziploc bags we had mailed ourselves in each resupply, fill the bag with water and Dr. Bronner's soap, toss in one of the diaper covers with the cloth inserts, and then shake vigorously for thir-

---

2. We brought dry wipes and added water when needed.

ty seconds. We'd pour out the water, wring out the diaper, and then put it back in the bag, rinsing it with just water for another thirty seconds. After wringing it out once more, we'd attach the diaper to the back of the pack with a safety pin, leaving it there to dry as we hiked. The cloth material of the diapers is thick, but when exposed to wind and sunlight would dry out within a day—and on the warmest of days, in a matter of hours.

If you're going to wash diapers along the trail, it's important to follow Leave No Trace guidelines. You are dealing with fecal matter, so it's important not to contaminate the water source. I would suggest getting water and then moving at least one hundred feet away before washing, ideally more.

One thing to note is that this diaper strategy works best west of the Mississippi River in the arid climate of the West. East of the Mississippi (as well as in parts of the Pacific Northwest), there is a lot more precipitation and higher humidity levels, which could result in diapers taking a lot longer to dry depending on the time of year. I have heard of thru-hikers on the Appalachian Trail using compostable diapers. While I'm skeptical that these diapers decompose within a few years, something like that would be worth looking into. It could also work to follow the same strategy as illustrated above, but with a greater quantity of each item—i.e., bring more disposables and reusables to account for rainy days and potentially longer drying times.

Clothing for Babies and Toddlers

The approach is the same as with adults—you are looking for something that will keep them comfortable and protected from the elements. I provide a more thorough gear list later in this section, but here are a few general suggestions first:

- We figured a rainsuit to be essential and brought along

one made by Tuffo.

- If you're carrying your child, they won't be moving as much nor will they necessarily be as warm as you. We brought an insulated jacket with a hood, a warm hat, mittens, wool booties, and a wool onesie for when temperatures really dropped.

- Wearing layers works just as well for kids as it does for adults. If it was windy, we'd often add Din's rainsuit on top of her warm-weather gear for further protection.

- Din's clothes were a mix of fast-wicking material and cotton. Yes, I know. "Cotton kills," but the PCT travels through a very arid environment, and we were able to put her in our clothes if hers got wet. This happened a couple times—Din would wear Alana's thick wool socks as pants or Alana's wool pullover as a dress.

- "Two is one and one is none." I'd plan for diaper leaks and accidents, so don't bring only one pair of pants and one shirt. For Din, we carried two pairs of pants, two T-shirts, one long-sleeved shirt, one insulated jacket, her rainsuit, two pairs of socks, mittens, wool and neoprene booties, and a winter hat. Again, besides diapers, this was all we brought for her.

- Your kid will likely get themselves and their clothes dirty—very dirty. If you find yourself worrying about keeping things pristine, you will become extremely frustrated.

Shoes

Perhaps the most important item of gear on the trail is footwear. With tens of thousands of steps each day for months, good footwear is a necessity. The lightweight backpacking revolution ushered in a wave of new ideas, including what you put on your feet. Gone were the cumbersome boots, weighing multiple pounds per pair. In their stead came trail runners—lightweight shoes (often around just a pound or less per shoe) that allow for greater comfort and breathability. Over the years, many people have switched over from the traditional style of boots, wowing themselves with their newfound quickness, comfort, and absence of foot issues. The old adage "A pound on your feet is worth five pounds on your back" has played out time and again, and with each boot often weighing 2 to 3 pounds or more, hikers end up "saving" 10 to 20 pounds total in weight. Extrapolated over 2,650 miles, this makes quite a difference.

Alana and I were fully on board with this mindset, having switched over to trail runners years ago. We take them everywhere—through Alaska's alpine ridges, snowfields, tundra, and swamps—so using them on a mostly dry trail was a no-brainer. Each pair typically lasts about 600 miles, with the insoles wearing flat after about 500 miles or so. Since we were planning on hiking for 4.5 to 5 months, we didn't want to put our gear to the limit and risk blowouts, so we decided to switch pairs roughly every 500 miles. Another reason it's better to be liberal with regards to changing pairs is that a hard trail with thin insoles makes for a constant, heavy impact on your feet and can cause pain and/or lead to injury.

The most popular shoes we saw on the PCT were Altra Lone Peaks. Their wide foot box allows for plenty of room for your toes and is a godsend for those with wide feet. These shoes retail new at $140 for men and $90 for women. Switching pairs every 500 miles meant that we'd each need 5 pairs. We weren't interested in paying close to four figures for shoes, so we looked for alternatives. I was able to source barely used shoes on eBay for an average of $52 a pair, while Alana found hers on Mercari for about $35 a pair. By foregoing pristine shoes, we each ended up spending only a third of what we would have otherwise, but still got shoes with minimal wear.

Our Gear

The following is our gear list from our trip. It does not list the clothing items Alana and I wore every day, which included shorts, underwear, t-shirts, socks, shoes, and sun hats. Some items, like pants, long underwear and Din's insulated onesie, weren't carried the whole trip and were only carried after we received our cold weather clothing in September. In addition to the items listed below, we were usually carrying four to five days' worth of food (at two pounds per person per day) and a couple liters of water.

Packs

- Osprey Poco Plus 126.2 ounces (oz)

- Hyperlite Mountain Gear Southwest 70L 36.0 oz

Sleep

- Therm-a-rest Z-Lite 3/4 sleeping pad 10.3 oz

- Therm-a-rest Z-Lite 3/4 sleeping pad 9.3 oz

- DIY Synthetic Double Quilt 30F 30.0 oz

- Seek Outside Silvertip Mid 30.0 oz

- Tent stakes 6.3 oz

Cooking

- MSR 1.3 Liter Pot 7.1 oz

- Wooden Spoon 1.0 oz

- Titanium Spoon 0.5 oz

- Stove 0.5 oz

- Aluminum Foil Windscreen 0.3 oz

- Fire Starting Kit 1.1 oz

- Knife 6.5 oz

- MSR Dromedary 6 Liters 9.2 oz

- Smartwater Bottles x3 1.0 oz

Clothing

- Grundens Rain Jacket 17.0 oz

- Black Diamond Rain Jacket 14.0 oz

- Montbell Synthetic Insulated Jacket 17.0 oz

- Montbell Synthetic Insulated Jacket 15.2 oz

- Alpaca Wool Hoody 10.9 oz

- Sherpa Fleece Pullover 30.0 oz

- PatagoniaWind Jacket 7.0 oz

- Black Diamond Wind Jacket 8.0 oz

- Alana Extra Underwear 6.5 oz

- Jack Extra Underwear 3.0 oz

- Alana Extra Socks 10.7 oz

- Alana Warm Hat 2.4 oz

- Jack Warm Hat 2.6 oz

- Fleece Headband 1.3 oz

- Mountain Hardwear AP Pants 36.7 oz

- Long underwear 5.0 oz

- Gloves x2 4.5 oz

- Headnet x2 2.0 oz

- Din Tuffo Rainsuit 6.9 oz

- Din Short Sleeve Shirts x2 4.1 oz

- Din Long Sleeve Shirt 2.0 oz

- Din Pants x2 8.0 oz

- Din Socks x2 1.0 oz

- Din Insulated Jacket 5.4 oz

- Din Wool Onesie 15.1 oz

- Din Wool Booties 1.0 oz

- Din Warm Hat 1.8 oz

- Din Mittens 1.0 oz

Toiletries/First Aid
- Water Filter (Steripen/Sawyer Squeeze) 8.0 oz

- Epipen 3.25 oz

- Benadryl 0.2 oz

- Ibuprofen 0.2 oz

- Aspirin 0.2 oz

- Sunscreen 3.0 oz

- Natural Bug Spray 2.0 oz

- Cloth Diapers and Inserts 34.5 oz

- Disposable Diapers (5) 5.5 oz

- Disposable Dry Wipes 12/day 1.0 oz

- Bamboo liners 0.5 oz

- Diaper Rash Powder 3.0 oz

- Moleskin Tape 1.0 oz

- Alcohol Pads 0.1 oz

- Imodium (anti-diarrhea) 0.2 oz

- Toothbrush x2 1.2 oz

- Toothpaste 2.0 oz

- Dr. Bronner Liquid Soap 2.7 oz

- Hand Sanitizer 2.7 oz

- Infant Meds (Zyrtec and Tylenol) 1.0 oz

Electronics
- iPhone SE 2020 7.5 oz

- iPhone SE 2020 6.7 oz

- 10,000 mAh Battery Bank 10.1 oz

- inReach Satellite Messaging Device 8.1 oz

- Browning Headlamp 4.1 oz

- Ultralight Headlamp 0.9 oz

- Charger Cables 3.0 oz

Acknowledgements

Our journey wouldn't have been possible without the help of so many loved ones. I am grateful to the many people who helped us along the way. Elizabeth Fernandez, who kindly housed our resupply boxes, took care of our gear, and spent months regularly going to the post office to get us our food on time. Chris Ferguson, who generously offered us a tremendous amount of encouragement and help from the moment he heard about our trip, including adding Remi to the gang for months. Tash Stickney, who arguably took on a greater adventure than our own, graciously leaving the splendor of the Big Apple to rough it in our cabin and take care of Remi on short notice. Andrew and Eva Allaby, who offered not only inspiration, but encouragement, advice, and help throughout the trip. Jayce Williamson, who shared her sewing machine and gave us advice when we didn't know a bobbin from a bumble bee. Cade Kellam, who charitably lent us his water filter and sense of humor on the rough days. Claire Montgomerie, who in her usual way helped us out in our hour of need despite having a full plate herself. Dorothy O'Donnell, Doug Amidon, and Chris Cramer for believing in us early and prodding us forward. My mom, Sheila McClure-Workman, who taught Alana how to sew in an hour, helped us with logistics en route, and encouraged us along the way. Alana's mom, Sandra Stickney, who consistently offered help and encouragement. Tyler Lau, who provided us with resources that made planning, logistics, and navigation far easier than they otherwise would have been. Michelle and Ed Averbuch, Marty McClure, Molly McClure, and Colin McClure for cheering us on. Kayla Johnson, for her constant encouragement and, as always, willingness to talk my wife off the ledge, whenever needed.

We are thankful to the many others who helped us after we got underway. The volunteers at the Washington Alpine Club, who made us feel at home with their delicious meals and welcoming accommodations. Delia in Carson, who took us into town in lieu of going hiking with her family. Karen in Carson, who benevolently bought us two full grocery bags of food. Martina and her son, who assisted us in our emergency and were kind enough to delay their plans to make sure we made it out okay. Joe, who lent a helping hand when it was most needed, helping facilitate communication and assistance. Kimberly and Chris, who made sure everything was alright and encouraged us along the way. The paramedic team at Lyons County, for accommodating us and insisting we continue on with our trip.

We are grateful to Vista for recovering Cheeks's lone jacket as well as for her friendship, which provided us with joy and comfort. Adam Christofferson, for the great company, encouragement, and allowing us to feel like something other than parents. Pierre, for being a source of laughter for Cheeks and putting up with nights of her crying.

We are indebted to Cody Markelz & Caryn Johansen and Tyler Disney, who each went above and beyond to help us out while en route, driving hours to pick us up and drop us off at trailheads, housing us, feeding us, and lending us gear. Dan and Charlotte Disney, for welcoming us into their home and sharing meals with us.

Jay Go, for generously providing us with a bear can. To all those who gave us rides along the way, including Leslie, Lynn, and the trail angel crew in Trout Lake. Devilfish, for providing water caches and giving hikers an opportunity to refuel when it's most needed. Sailor and Cookies, for the ride to town and for providing accommodations in what may be the best stop off the trail. The many people on the trail and in towns who offered us encouragement, motivating us to keep plodding southward.

One of the pleasures in writing out our adventure has been working with an incredible team of people to help put forward the best version of this book possible. I am thankful to all my early readers and the feedback they provided—Sheila McClure-Workman, Marty McClure, Molly McClure, Colin McClure, Tyler Disney, and Cody Markelz. Caryn Johansen, for her help brainstorming. Cody Markelz, yet again, for creating excellent complementary illustrations. My editor, Matt Samet, for his efficient work, clear communication, and help in simplifying the work and deliver a stronger text.

I am forever thankful to my dear wife, Alana, for being crazy enough to embark on this adventure with me, tough enough to forge through, and patient enough to work through whatever issue we faced. Beyond the trail, she played an integral part in the creation of this book, listening to my ideas, allowing me time to write and edit, and reviewing and providing feedback from early drafts to the final product. None of this would have been possible without her.

www.ingramcontent.com/pod-product-compliance
Lightning Source LLC
Chambersburg PA
CBHW022050020426
42335CB00012B/625